Praise for

TINY LEAPS, BIG CHANGES

"I love Gregg's philosophy on changing your life: It's all about adjusting your day-to-day behavior. This book is a clear, concise guide for doing just that. Go create the life you deserve!"

   —Jason Feifer, editor-in-chief, *Entrepreneur* Magazine

"This is not a self-help book—this is a playbook for making real change in your life, one small step at a time. I highly recommend it!"

   —Ryan Carson, founder and CEO of Treehouse

"Refreshingly honest and REAL! A step-by-step guide to achieving anything you want. I'd recommend [*Tiny Leaps, Big Changes*] for anyone wanting to move forward in their mindset, strategy, and goals!"

   —Erika De La Cruz, TV host, bestselling author

TINY
LEAPS
BIG CHANGES

TINY
LEAPS
BIG CHANGES

GREGG CLUNIS

Everyday Strategies to Accomplish More, Crush
Your Goals, and Create the Life You Want

CENTER
STREET

NEW YORK NASHVILLE

Center Street
Hachette Book Group
1290 Avenue of the Americas, New York, NY 10104

centerstreet.com

twitter.com/centerstreet

First Trade Paperback Edition: January 2019

Center Street is a division of Hachette Book Group, Inc.
The Center Street name and logo are trademarks of Hachette Book Group, Inc.

The publisher is not responsible for websites (or their content) that are not owned by the publisher.

The Hachette Speakers Bureau provides a wide range of authors for speaking events. To find out more, go to www.HachetteSpeakersBureau.com or call (866) 376-6591.

Library of Congress Cataloging-in-Publication Data
Names: Clunis, Gregg, author.
Title: Tiny leaps, big changes / by Gregg Clunis.
Description: New York: Center Street, [2019]
Identifiers: LCCN 2018026389| ISBN 9781546082750 (trade pbk.) |
    ISBN 9781549113321 (audio download) | ISBN 9781546082767 (ebook)
Subjects: LCSH: Change (Psychology) | Self-realization.
Classification: LCC BF637.C4 C58 2019 | DDC 158.1—dc23
LC record available at https://lccn.loc.gov/2018026389

ISBNs: 978-1-5460-8275-0 (trade paperback), 978-1-5460-8276-7 (ebook)

Printed in the United States of America

LSC-C

10 9 8 7 6 5 4 3 2 1

For Hopeton and Rose. This book is possible only because of the sacrifices you've made and the risks you've taken. I am who I am today because of you. Thank you.

CONTENTS

PART III
How to Keep Moving Forward

THE STORY OF IMMIGRANTS

Life is a series of natural and spontaneous changes. Don't resist them; that only creates sorrow. Let reality be reality. Let things flow naturally forward in whatever way they like.

—*Lao-Tzu*

On December 26, 2000, my family and I moved to the United States. I was seven years old, and I hadn't seen my dad for roughly nine months.

My family had been separated, not because we didn't want to be together, but because my parents were choosing to make an enormous change. One that would affect the direction of our lives forever.

At the time, the economy was in a tough place. Work was scarce, money was tight, and opportunities were limited. In response, my parents made the bold decision to sell everything they owned, pack a few bags, and move their family to a new country. Yup, we were heading from the small island of Jamaica to the land of opportunity: the United States of America.

When you make a major change like this, you can't just jump into it and expect good results—it takes planning, groundwork, and a whole lot of trust. My parents decided that my father would go to the States a few months ahead of us in order to secure a job and find a place to live. Once he had accomplished that goal, he would send for us and we'd be reunited. Seems easy, right? I was too young at the time to understand what was happening during that period in our lives, but I knew it wasn't easy—it was *really* difficult.

There is not a single person on the planet who wants to be separated from the people they love, especially not for months on end. But my parents had a specific goal in mind, an outcome they wanted, and they knew that sacrifice was required in order to accomplish it.

Nine months later, we were reunited, but the struggle was nowhere close to finished. Over the next eighteen years, my mother and father would sacrifice over and over again to ensure that our family could survive and make things work. This story isn't uncommon. In fact, it's been played out millions of times. Scrappy immigrants leave their country for the land of opportunity, work hard, contribute to society, and find the life they were looking for. It's the entire basis of the American dream.

The brave people who pursue that American dream don't get enough credit. When you pack up and move for a better life, you essentially start over with nothing: no money, no social capital, few friendships, and no connection to your local community. The obstacles in front of a newly minted immigrant are huge. If you are willing to face them, it's likely because you have a strong reason.

For my parents, that reason was me and my sister, Sherri-Ann, who was just about to graduate from high school. They knew that the financial and career opportunities in the States could benefit us both and so they took actions to make them available to us. Thanks to their hard work, I never wanted for much. Everything I needed was taken care of, and being the younger child, I can assure you that my family would say I was spoiled. I was, but I also saw firsthand what it cost my parents to be able to spoil me.

Growing up watching their struggle, their willingness to deal with it, and the results it has produced taught me a fundamental lesson about the world: that while not everyone will be a millionaire or have a six-pack or find the love of their life, everyone is capable of setting a clear goal and taking the actions required to move toward it. It's this experience that drives my current life philosophy, my podcast, and now this book.

All big changes in your life come from the tiny leaps you take every day.

Tiny leaps every single day are what my parents took after they made the decision that they would leave Jamaica. Tiny leaps every single day are what allowed them, after arriving here, to work twelve-hour days and overnight shifts—at the cost of time with their kids. Tiny leaps every single day are what allowed them to recover, both financially and emotionally, after working hard to buy a house, only to lose it during the height of the Great Recession.

You may be reading this book because you are looking for some secret knowledge to help you achieve everything you've ever wanted. Perhaps you've read countless personal development books for the same reason and thought, *Maybe this one will finally tell me the secret to changing my life.*

Well, you're right. This book does contain the secret to changing your life, and I'm going to reveal it to you.

Are you ready?

The secret to changing your life in any area is to set a clear goal, audit the behaviors you engage in each day, and then make changes to those behaviors to make progress toward that goal.

This focus on goal setting and day-to-day behavioral modification has allowed immigrants from all around the world to leave their country, start with nothing, and build comfortable lives.

This focus has allowed men and women to come from humble means and rise to the heights of Olympic championship, even when the odds were against them.

This focus has allowed self-made entrepreneurs to build massive wealth, create livelihoods for others, and bring value to the marketplace, all while simultaneously changing the world around them.

But you already knew that, didn't you?

You know that if you want to be healthier, you simply need to clarify your goal, audit your diet and exercise behaviors, and then make changes. You know that if you want to make more money, all it requires is being straightforward about it, looking at your behaviors at work or in your spare time, and making changes to move you toward higher pay.

You know all of this.

So my question is, why are you reading yet another self-help book in search of an answer you already have?

The truth is that you picked up this book because it's easier to keep searching for an answer than it is to take action. Reading self-help books gives you the impression of being productive when, really, it's just another form of procrastination. We all do it. The good news is, this is not a self-help book.

The self-help and personal development industries have

made the act of self-improvement far more complicated than it actually is. We learn about things like "manifesting" and "The Secret," and we end up thinking that the process of changing our lives is something special and unattainable. The result is that there are millions of people out there who don't pay any attention to self-improvement. They hear the lingo, see the cultlike community, and immediately shut out the message.

So I say that this is not self-help because it isn't—it's your daily life and the natural human instinct to move one step forward each day.

Throughout this book, you won't hear a single peep about "manifesting" your future. What you'll see instead is a simple framework for how to look at your life, decide what you want, and take the actions that move you toward that reality.

You won't be told to find your passion or follow your dreams. Instead I'll talk about the flaws of passion, why the pursuit of it might be doing more damage than it's worth, and what you should follow instead. There will be no jargon, no exclusivity, and no "us against them" mentality. All you'll find in this book is practical advice on what is required to create change in your life.

So without further ado, grab a cup of coffee and get ready for the ride, because you are now reading *Tiny Leaps, Big Changes*.

PART I

HOW TO CHANGE YOUR LIFE

CHAPTER ONE

WHAT IS CHANGE?

The only way that we can live is if we grow. The only way that we can grow is if we change. The only way that we can change is if we learn. The only way we can learn is if we are exposed. And the only way that we can become exposed is if we throw ourselves out into the open. Do it. Throw yourself.

—*C. JoyBell C.*

A little over three years ago, while living in Washington Heights, a neighborhood in Manhattan, I stumbled across a networking event called Thrive Dinners. They were peculiar events where, each month, a few dozen twenty-somethings would get together in a food court to talk, meet new people, and share what they were most excited about in their careers. I only ever attended three events, but they were always packed with some of the most interesting people I've ever met.

The first time I went, I didn't really know anyone, and I'll be honest, I was nervous. I'd been to networking events in the city before, but they were usually pretty frustrating experiences filled with lawyers and accountants trying to bring me on as a client. Not exactly my scene. It seemed like Thrive Dinners would be exactly the same, and being alone made it much worse.

So there I was, by myself, at a random networking event, with nothing interesting to discuss. In search of someone to talk to, I stumbled over to a table that didn't seem too packed. In front of me sat a guy with messy brown hair wearing a patterned button-up shirt with the top two buttons undone. He had a pretty relaxed vibe about him, which made it much easier for me to approach him and say hello.

This is how I met Matt Kohn.

He was what some might consider a modern hippie—all about peace, love, positivity, and parties. That's how I would have described him. But throughout our conversation, he regularly spoke about the business ideas he had and the blog he wanted to start. He asked me about my projects and listened with a keen interest. He showed a genuine excitement for what others were doing and asked questions to learn more. By the time our conversation ended, it was made clear that he didn't just want more from his life—he was starving for it.

A few months later, he sent me a Facebook message saying, "Change of plans. I might move to Medellín, Colombia." Eighteen months later came a new life update: Matt lives in Colombia for roughly six months of the year, he's met a girl he describes to me as "the love of his life," and he runs his dream company, a digital agency called Different Hunger Media.

If you look at his story on the surface, it might seem like a typical overnight success. He was frustrated at his job, decided to quit and follow his passion, and was successful. You might say, "Well, he just got lucky, I couldn't do that." Or you might even say, "Some people are just able to do stuff like that. I certainly can't."

The problem with both of these statements is that they are only half right. You would be right in saying that you probably wouldn't find the exact success that he's found. After all, even if you took the exact same actions, your life and situation are still different from his. But you'd be wrong in thinking that he just got "lucky." If Matt got "lucky," it was purely because he chose to create that luck at the expense of everything else. It seems like he made a major leap in his life, completely disrupted his norm, and found success in his risk, but by the end of this chapter, I think you'll agree that his success came from small, incremental steps each and every day—steps that started well before he and I had ever met.

In order to prove this, we need to break down Matt's choices, but first, we'll need a framework for what change looks like and how we each experience it. Then we'll apply that framework to Matt's story and see how it plays out.

THE SIX STAGES OF PERSONAL CHANGE

Over the last two years, 280-plus episodes of my podcast, and massive amounts of time researching and thinking about how change happens in an individual's life, I've made many attempts to identify what exactly change looks like. After all, it seems silly that we all want to change our lives, but most of us don't even know what that would mean.

Here's my hypothesis, developed after countless conversations with people far more qualified than I over the last two years: Each person's experience of change is different, but the psychological aspects of that change are more or less the same.

To better understand what I mean, think of the Five Stages of Grief by Elisabeth Kübler-Ross and David Kessler.[1] You and I may have a different personal experience with grief, but according to their model, the stages we go through are similar regardless of how they present themselves.

The same holds true for any kind of change, so allow me to introduce you to the Six Stages of Personal Change, a model I pieced together that represents a step-by-step process we must each go through when trying to change our lives.

Stage One: Inspiration

"Hey, just so you know, work starts at 9:00 a.m."

It was 9:45 a.m., and thanks to various delays on New York City's subway system, I found myself sprinting out of the subway and across two intersections just to make it into work—forty-five minutes late. This wasn't something I did often. I usually tried to be on time, but this day was not shaping up to be a good one, and to make matters worse, I now had to endure a series of passive-aggressive comments from my boss about tardiness. I'm not sure why this one infraction incurred his wrath; my only guess is that it was either a serious issue, one worthy of bringing up, or that he was having a bad morning and needed to get out his own frustrations.

Whatever it was, the comments left a bad taste in my mouth. I knew I was a good employee, that I worked hard to bring value to the company, and that the ideas I brought to the table were directly benefiting our bottom line. If this had been an isolated incident, I'm sure I would have just gotten over it and dealt with my failure, but thanks to the ever-present negativity of our work environment, this experience quickly turned into my last straw.

Naturally, I spent the next few days looking and applying for new jobs on my lunch break. After all, if my boss wasn't going to appreciate the work I did, I would find a different company that would.

Does this sound familiar? The first piece of the puzzle when it comes to changing our lives is something we experience often: frustration. Each of us has something in our lives that causes it. It may be a job we dislike, friendships we no longer benefit from, a lack of finances, how we feel when we look in the mirror...Whatever it may be, if used correctly, that frustration can become a catalyst for creating change. We naturally try to do what we can to move away from frustration and toward something that better fits what we are looking for.

So then why is it that we don't all change our lives every single time we feel frustrated? Because there is another piece of the puzzle that needs to be in place: a moment of inspiration that is strong enough to open our minds to other options.

Here's the difference: You might get frustrated at your

job. Maybe your boss is asking too much of you and isn't willing to pay you a fair salary in order to get it, or maybe it's just not a challenging environment. For most of us, it ends there. We have a moment of frustration and then we suck it up and stick with the program.

But what if right at the moment you felt frustrated with your job, you heard about a former coworker who was just as frustrated as you but chose to quit three months ago and is now doing work they love? Or what if you were to stumble across a video about how one of your role models had hit rock bottom right before they got their break that allowed them to accomplish all of their dreams?

The inspiration you feel from either of these situations would give you just enough momentum to take the next step rather than fall back into the same pattern. Once you find that inspiration, you'll be able to move into Stage Two, which is all about exploring what options are available to you.

Stage Two: Curiosity

Once you've experienced the combination of being frustrated by your current situation and being inspired to make a change, you'll naturally start to ask, "What else is out there?"

This is the stage where someone starts searching through job listings, checking out diets, or looking for ways to make money from home. At this point, you aren't quite ready to commit, but you are weighing your options and trying to imagine yourself in a different place. This is a necessary step in the process and shouldn't be rushed.

Your goal during this stage should simply be to experience everything you can. You need to see what is out there, what it's like, and decide whether or not something could be a good direction for you. The problem is that for most people who make it to this stage, it's the end of the road. Searching for options creates a feeling of progress, even if none is actually there. This false feeling could derail your search by providing your brain with some of the short-term benefits that are associated with changing your situation.

For example, when you get frustrated at work and start searching for new job opportunities, you may start to feel like you've made progress because you looked at five or six listings and even applied for one or two of them. That feeling undermines the difficult process of making a real change and could end in your falling back into the routine of everyday life before you know it. This is a *huge* problem if your goal is to actually change your life. Beyond that, there is another potential trap: setting this stage as the goal itself.

Let's say you get frustrated at work. That night you

cook yourself a nice meal, pour yourself a glass of your favorite wine, and start looking into other jobs. The next morning, you may not even remember why you were frustrated. Instead you just remember that you had a pleasant evening.

This happens because of something called the *fading affect bias,*[2] also known as FAB. According to *Wikipedia*, FAB is "a psychological phenomenon in which information regarding negative emotions tends to be forgotten more quickly than that associated with pleasant emotions." You were frustrated at work but the next morning you are more likely to remember the nice evening you had. This can be good for everyday life, but if you really want to leave your job, it can get in the way by downplaying your frustrations, which makes it harder to use them to your advantage. With that said, if you can avoid these pitfalls in Stage Two and manage to make it to Stage Three, you'll be over the two major sticking points in this process and on your way to finally creating the change you've always wanted.

Stage Three: Connection

You'll come across a lot of options in Stage Two. Many will seem great, others will seem impossible, but before you can start to change your life, you first need to find an option that feels right and excites you while simultaneously seeming doable. You need to identify with the new option; otherwise you'll never feel as though it's possible.

Here's what I mean: Let's say you are currently a single mother of three young children and you make decent money, but with three kids and many bills to take care of alone, it gets really tough to keep everything together. You work really hard, so one day you decide to ask for a raise from your boss. She says no and gives you a list of reasons that don't make sense to you. That's a pretty frustrating moment.

But you don't let it stop you. Instead of feeling bad for yourself, you decide to look for new ways to make a bit more money. Eventually you hear someone talking about how they quit their job, opened their own retail store, and now make twice as much as they did before. How do you think you'd react?

That's great for them, but I can't really do that.

Where would I even get the money to start it?

This must be a scam.

I'm not smart enough for something like that.

This is what I call *self-doubt alarms*. They're the dreaded inner voice that tells you that "you're not good enough" regardless of your abilities. The truth is that you may be perfectly capable of achieving something similar, but that isn't what matters. What matters most in this stage is finding something that will actually move you to action, and the only way this happens is to feel connected to the path. If the path you stumble across seems too far out of reach, you won't recognize your potential; therefore, you'll never take action to make it happen.

This is why an option like opening a retail store will immediately trigger your self-doubt alarms, while a similar job at a different company feels attainable. They are both possibilities, but opening a retail store seems a million miles away, while being in a similar position somewhere new is only a few tiny leaps away. Your goal in this stage should be either to identify a new option that is just a few steps ahead of where you are or to find an option that has a clear path toward it. By doing so, you'll have a much higher chance of taking action and moving yourself into the next stage.

Stage Four: Discovery

If you've made it to Stage Four, you are probably bursting with energy, excitement, and enthusiasm for what lies ahead. Why shouldn't you be? Getting to Stage Four means you've identified something you aren't satisfied with, taken the necessary steps to identify other options, and actually found something that resonates with you. You've probably even started to take small steps toward making your desired change possible—maybe you've started cutting back on fast food and are choosing some healthier options. Perhaps you've taken the time to create a budget that you intend on following. Maybe all you've done so far is spend some time deciding your next steps, checking out books, articles, videos, podcasts, communities, and any other resources you can find on your subject. Of course, these resources have been there all along, but in this stage, they will become relevant. That's what Stage Four is all about.

It's actually quite interesting why this happens. The culprit is a weird little trick that our brain plays called *sensory gating*.[3] From *Wikipedia*: "Sensory gating describes neurological processes of filtering out redundant or unnecessary stimuli in the brain from all possible environmental stimuli. Also referred to as gating or filtering, sensory gating prevents an overload of irrelevant information in the higher cortical centers of the brain."

Basically, it's a fancy way of saying that the brain is constantly filtering out irrelevant information from your environment to ensure you don't go crazy. Your brain has been filtering out all those resources because they weren't important to your life, but now that you are paying attention, your brain will let them into your world.

Here's an example of how it works: Let's say that you

want to improve your relationship with your spouse. The first thing you might do is start looking for articles on the subject to give you some direction. The next day, you're walking out of your favorite coffee shop when you notice someone reading a book all about relationship advice. Later, as you drive home from work, the radio plays an ad for an upcoming event featuring a relationship expert.

In the moment, it seems like fate that these things just happened to pop up after you made the decision to fix your relationship; but this stuff was always there—your brain would just filter it out. Amazing, right? Finding these resources is important because, as you navigate Stage Five, you will rely on them to keep you moving forward when you feel the most frustrated, and are most likely to quit this entire process.

Stage Five: Tiny Leaps

The most important stage of this entire process is the actual day-to-day experience of changing your life. It's great if you figure out what you want to do, but without taking action each and every day to move you toward that goal, you will find yourself living in your head, daydreaming of future results. Simply put, your day-to-day behaviors are what create major changes in your life over time. If you reach this stage, don't discount tiny actions just because they don't seem as impactful as the larger one. The small things matter.

Is your goal to get in better shape? Did you struggle with eating healthy today? That's fine! Just incorporate an extra vegetable into your dinner.

Is your goal to make more money? Did you set a goal to gain a new skill by a certain date and now find yourself running behind? No worries! Spend five minutes on that skill tonight.

These small behaviors might seem inconsequential, but when we make tiny leaps, we start changing our psychology, and when we want to change our lives, most of what we struggle with falls into the category of *limiting psychology*.

Let's say I told you that you needed to go climb a mountain, but it's not something you've ever done before. You'd likely be terrified and might protest. Part of the reasoning will come from the perceived difficulty, but another part of the protest is coming from how you identify yourself. You don't think of yourself as someone who climbs mountains—it's just not a part of your identity. As a result, the challenge of climbing a mountain is going to be impossible even before you get to the base.

If, however, you were first given an introductory class on how to start climbing, and you went out and did an easy climb, all of a sudden the thought of having to summit a mountain might still seem difficult, but it will at least seem possible.

By pursuing tiny leaps in our life during Stage Five, we allow ourselves to adopt the identity of the type of person we want to become. If we want to be serious about going to the gym, we first need to start seeing ourselves as the type of person who goes to the gym. If we want to learn a new skill, we first need to overcome the hurdle of thinking that we could never acquire that skill.

This is all about execution. You've got the inspiration, you know what you want to do, you've discovered the resources required to get you there, now all you have to do is commit and execute the small things every day that will move you toward your goal. It's definitely not a straight line—in fact, you'll spend more time sliding backward than going forward—but during this stage, you need to focus exclusively on keeping your head down and taking one tiny leap at a time.

Stage Six: Repeat

The really interesting thing about changing your life is that the process doesn't end.

You'll never actually leave Stage Five. Instead, you'll continue the process of taking tiny leaps every single day until you reach your goal. Once there, the goal will change and you'll take tiny leaps every single day until you reach your new goal.

I know—not the fairytale ending you wanted, right? You've worked so hard, why shouldn't you get to stop? Well, you can if you'd like, but the world around you won't stop moving forward, and if you aren't moving forward with it, you may wake up one day to find yourself in the same place you were when you started this process.

Additionally, owing to the nature of making small changes each and every day rather than major changes, you likely won't even realize when you've hit the goal you set out to reach. Changes will come naturally over time, and you'll quickly adjust to them. They'll become your new norm, and your eyes will continue to aim forward.

You might be wondering, "If I'm never supposed to leave Stage Five, why not just leave out Stage Six entirely?" Aside from the fact that six sounds infinitely better than five, it's worth reminding you that you should be aiming to start a life-long process of continual improvement. The journey itself is the goal, and anything else you accomplish on the way is a bonus. Any change you achieve in your life will always be replaced with another pursuit. That is the nature of human beings.

The point of this framework isn't to achieve your goal and then walk away; it's to continually pursue better, to always aim higher, and to focus on turning your daily behaviors into a lifestyle that you find rewarding regardless of the specific outcome.

It's the process my parents had to navigate when they decided to move their family to the United States and create a new life from scratch, it's the process I experience on a day-to-day basis in my pursuit of financial freedom, it's the process that virtually everyone we consider to be "successful" has had to navigate throughout their lives, and it's the process you'll need in order to make a change in your own life. The change you are trying to create in your own life may differ wildly from mine, but if you pay close attention to the steps you take, you'll notice that we're working off the same map.

Let's go back to Matt's story to see how he navigated this process during those pivotal stages of his transition from working full-time to moving to a new country and founding a digital agency that generates six figures in revenue every year.

INSPIRATION

When Matt and I first met, he had a long commute on busy subways to his office, a small cubicle, and all the frustrations that come with corporate life, so his moment of frustration and inspiration had already happened. He was already in Stage One.

When I reached out to him about this book, he had some trouble nailing down a specific moment in which he realized how frustrated he was, but it was certainly there. In his words:

I was a twenty-something professional working in New York City. Like many of my friends, I took the first job I was offered and proceeded to follow the path taken by 99 percent of my peers.

I was working as a consultant at a tech startup company. On paper, I had every reason to be happy. I was making a decent salary and had the privilege of living in one of the greatest cities in the world.

But I was restless inside. I was hungry for something more.

The problem was simple: I wasn't fulfilled by my work.

Not being fulfilled by our work is one of the most common causes of frustration in the workplace. This isn't true just for Millennials either. According to a 2013 study[4] performed by the compensation data tracking website Salary.com, only 38 percent of the Americans surveyed felt that they were personally fulfilled by the work they do.

Humans want to do great work. We want to matter and we want to work hard, but working in systems that don't accomplish anything of real value causes us to feel unfulfilled, which leads to frustration. According to Tony Robbins, the bestselling author and life coach known for working with everyone from elite athletes to Oprah to President Bill Clinton, the need for significance is one of the strongest desires that we, as humans, all share. It spans generations, and given that our work makes up such a large part of our lives, it naturally comes into play in our careers.

When I spoke with Matt further, he said the following:

I spent my weeks living for the weekends. As soon as Sunday rolled around, I dreaded Monday. My job wasn't miserable, but I was miserable knowing I was spending the most important years of my life in a job that didn't fulfill me.

Luckily, Matt didn't fall into the Stage One trap by endlessly cycling between frustration and normalcy. Instead, he felt the pull of inspiration and decided to take action.

CURIOSITY

This is where I first entered the story. Stage Two is all about figuring out what your options are, and one of the best ways to do that is to get into the world and talk to people, which was part of Matt's motivation for being at the Thrive Dinner that night. He knew he wanted to do something, he had the seeds of an idea, but the only thing that could help him solidify his direction and connect with a new path was to be exposed to others who were doing exactly what he wanted or better.

Jim Rohn, quite possibly the most quoted man in the personal development field, once said, "You are the average of the five people you spend the most time with." The idea here is simple: The people you surround yourself with dictate the types of conversations you have, and those dictate the realm of ideas and possibilities that you think about, and those thoughts dictate your actions.

What Matt was trying to do—and I highly recommend that we all follow his lead—was surround himself with people doing the type of thing he wanted to do. The people he met at this event expanded his understanding of his options and helped him figure out which path to follow. People who, at the time, ran web design firms from Medellín, Colombia, and spent their spare time traveling the world were huge inspirations for Matt.

Of course, being exposed to new options isn't what's important—it's connecting with one that changes the game.

CONNECTION

Many of the people Matt met at this event belonged to a subculture known as digital nomads, a group of individuals who embrace remote-based work, or start a remote-based business in order to become location independent. This means they can earn an income from anywhere in the world that has a Wi-Fi connection, so they often travel and settle down in countries like Colombia and Thailand, where the value of a single US dollar can get them far more than it can in the United States. It's an interesting way of living that was originally made popular by Tim Ferriss in his book *The 4-Hour Workweek*.[5]

It's possible that Matt already knew about the digital nomad option prior to leaving his job, but the people he met in Stage Two helped him connect with this path for his own life. By being around them, having conversations, and getting his questions answered, he was able to better understand what was involved, ultimately helping him come to the decision that it made more financial sense to quit his job and change countries than to quit his job and stay in New York City, one of the most expensive places in the world.

This represented a connection with his new path. He

always knew that he could quit his job and start a business, but owing to the high cost of living in New York City, it was more difficult to accomplish that confidently. After being exposed to the digital nomad lifestyle, he reconnected with his desire to make it happen.

DISCOVERY

This stage was an important one for Matt. Before he left New York City, moved to Colombia, and went full-time on his business, he wasn't capable of building the kind of business he wanted. He didn't have the experience, skills, resources, or any of the things one might expect an entrepreneur to have. But thanks to the first three stages, he did know exactly what he wanted to do and found a way to make it possible.

His only job at this point was to take action and start building with an open mind and a willingness to ask for help. What happened next started a chain reaction that changed his life forever.

First, he found resources on how to land his first few clients in order to start making a few bucks from his web design services. Next, he learned how to outsource some of his development work to make himself more scalable. Then, he learned how to sell more effectively, how to create the systems required to run a business, how to set up a business structure and hire his first employee...the list goes on.

The point is that, at every step of the process, he found the resources he needed to help him navigate it. That's the beauty: You don't need to know everything prior to starting. Matt didn't begin this journey with the skills or resources required to build and run a digital agency that generates six figures in revenue—he simply decided that he wanted to change, explored his options, found something he connected with, and allowed himself to find the resources he needed.

TINY LEAPS

For the first nine months of Matt's life as an entrepreneur, he struggled. He wasn't bringing in enough revenue, he was stuck doing work that he didn't like, and he was genuinely unhappy with what he had built. He found himself in thousands of dollars of credit card debt, consistently working fifty to sixty hours per week, and barely getting by each month. This was when he decided to start this process over and make another change. He was frustrated with his situation, identified the option he wanted to pursue, and brought in resources in the form of a coach.

As a result, he paid off his debt and went on to sell

$90,000 in new business, making him the owner of a six-figure revenue agency. All of that is fantastic but here's the really important part: None of that would have been possible had he not taken some small steps toward personal change in the beginning. Without the nine months of frustration as an entrepreneur, he would not have made the second change required to jump to the next level. Each step of the way connected to the next one from the day he first experienced frustration with his job to where he is now.

The two realities are vastly different, but the steps in between had to be experienced in order to make the end result possible. Matt's secret was consistent action in the direction he wanted to go, and a willingness to adapt as he slowly became the person he wanted to be.

REPEAT

To this day, Matt is still navigating this process and aiming even higher than he could have imagined just a few years ago. He is navigating this cycle constantly as he changes his goals, finds new resources, and determines new paths to pursue.

The Six Stages of Personal Change are a continuous process that each of us experiences. Whether we choose to consciously change our life or not is irrelevant; we are all following this process as it relates to the areas of our life that go through change.

So you might be thinking, "Well, if I'm following this process regardless, why am I not seeing anything change?"

The issue is that most of us never get past the cyclical nature of Stage One.

THE TRAP OF FRUSTRATION

As I mentioned earlier, we all get frustrated at certain points in life. No matter how much you've accomplished, you will always feel frustration. This happens because humans are wired for continual progress. We want to move forward, and so once we accomplish something, the goal posts get shifted.

But here's an idea that will throw you off a bit: The reason most of us don't move past that stage of frustration is because humans, in general, are also shockingly capable of accepting things just as they are. Even worse, we are incredibly capable of adapting to new things, even if they're negative. I know—those two ideas seem contradictory, right? How is it that we are both wired for the pursuit of progress and capable of accepting things as they are? There are two essential psychological biases that are responsible for this strange relationship.

The first is called the *status quo bias*. According to Rob Henderson, a student at Yale University and a research assistant at the Yale Mind and Development Lab, "When individuals are faced with the choice to change their environment or remain in their current state of affairs...most will choose the familiar. It is likely that this is a form of risk aversion that is characteristic of status quo bias—that individuals averse to the risk of losing their current reality will choose to remain..."[6]

The status quo bias perfectly explains our preference to stick with what we know as opposed to embracing the new and unknown, even if that means a positive change. Status quo bias is the reason we tend to avoid change at all costs; it just feels much better, and easier, to hold on to what we already have rather than risk losing it just for the chance of gaining something else. So status quo bias explains why we tend to avoid change, but what about our desire to seek progress?

For this piece of the puzzle, let's look at something called the *variability selection hypothesis*. First presented by paleoanthropologist Rick Potts in 1998, this hypothesis essentially claims that, owing to massive shifts in environmental and climate conditions that our early ancestors had to endure, our species has gained the ability for massive plasticity over time through evolution.

The harsh, dry, hot environment of pre-settled Australia was at the opposite end of the spectrum when compared to the cold of Northern Europe. Nevertheless, the remains of early *Homo sapiens* can be found in both regions. How is that possible? How can the same species thrive in environments that are extreme on opposite ends?

The variability selection hypothesis[7] simply states that natural selection allowed us to develop the brains required to make it work. We are not perfectly suited to any particular kind of area; instead we are somewhere in the middle and able to survive, even if not comfortably, in most environments found on earth.

In addition, humans have the most advanced brains on the planet—ones capable of changing our surroundings in order to make the world more hospitable to our needs. When you combine these two pieces together, you start to form a picture of why we tend to consistently pursue progress. Progress and change are the only things we are naturally adept at creating because it's the only way that our species could survive.

But let's get back to the point. The combination of our desire to hold on to what we have and our natural tendency to change ourselves and the world around us has allowed us to thrive as a species and rise to the top of the food chain despite our physical limitations as compared to other species. It's really quite an impressive feat when you consider it. But this is why changing your life feels scary. You want to do it, you know you need to do it, but you are afraid of the risks that naturally come with change. If you can better understand these two forces, they will allow you to take the actions required to make changes despite how scary they may feel.

Knowing that you feel an aversion to the action simply because you are biased toward staying the same, and also knowing that you are capable of quickly adapting to any massive change that may come, will give you the psychological freedom to take actions and actually start to see some of the good things you've always wanted.

However, none of this will be possible if you are unable to escape the trap of frustration. Sure, the status quo bias might explain why we can get frustrated every single day and choose to do nothing about it, but it doesn't tell us much about how we escape the cycle—that's what the Six Stages are meant to help us accomplish.

You now know what the process of change looks like. You know that Stage One is a trap that most people quickly fall into. You also know that you are *naturally* capable of navigating any change because of your unique ability to adapt and make it your new normal, and then hold on to that new normal for fear of losing it. By being aware of what factors are involved in creating the trap in the first place, you can push yourself out of the trap of Stage One.

In order to change your life, you must force it. Not through strength or stubbornness, but by consciously creating the environment to enable seamless navigation through the process.

CHAPTER TWO

WHAT DO YOU WANT?

Very often you are getting what you are asking for,
you're just not aware of how generally you are asking.

—*Tony Robbins*

In the winter of 2016, Ashlee Fazio, a then twenty-four-
year-old college graduate living in upstate New York,
made what many would consider to be a risky, irrespon-
sible, and downright foolish decision.

She bought a house. It was a real fixer-upper so she
spent a few months investing everything she had into
renovating the space and getting it ready for move-in.
Once it was good to go, she packed up all of her things
and moved in full-time. You might be thinking, *What's
the big deal? She's twenty-four—she should be moving out,
and good for her for buying a house!*

Well, her new home was a bit different than what you might be picturing. For starters, there was no living room, dining room, or bedroom. The entire home was only about 160 square feet, and along the outside of the structure, you could find four wheels and a hitch attached to it.

Ashlee's new home was a tiny house on wheels.

She'd been considering this move for a few years. Tiny homes were cheaper than regular ones, they weren't restricted to any singular area, and they were, at least in her mind, the first step to a life of *wanderlust* and financial freedom.

Then finally, in 2016, she decided to take the plunge and make it happen.

She wasn't sure how it would go or where it would take her, but those things didn't matter. She knew that she wanted the freedom to travel and her own space, and she wanted to keep her living expenses as low as possible in order to earn true financial freedom. A move that, to many looking from the outside, seemed reckless and silly was actually well thought out and, according to her a year later, one of the best things she's ever done.

There's an important lesson here: The only way to get what you want is to first *know* what it is that you want. So many of us spend the majority of our lives with no real idea of where we are trying to go. We wake up each day, go through our routine, worry about the small stuff, and then go to bed. Each day that passes is one less day we have, and one more spent wandering aimlessly. It's a problem. Without knowing where you're headed, you're simply floating down a river with no direction. Specificity and clarity are incredible pieces of the puzzle that allow you to build a map when it comes to your goals. You wouldn't go on a road trip without a clear idea of the place you want to end up, so why would you navigate life without a clear understanding of what it is you want?

Are you trying to get in shape? Ask yourself, what exactly do you want your body to look like? Maybe you're looking for a more fulfilling career? If that's the case, you need to ask yourself what kind of career would you like. Would you like to make more money? Great! But how much exactly?

Getting crystal clear about what kind of life you want to build is the very first step because it allows you to start moving in the right direction. Not knowing will leave you in the dark. Unfortunately, this is how most people live their lives, but that doesn't have to be how you do it. And just in case you still aren't convinced, one additional benefit of being clear about what it is you want for your life is that, as a consequence, you will also gain clarity on the kind of actions you should be taking and the kind of actions you should be avoiding.

This isn't to say that you need to sit down and plan out your entire life. That approach simply doesn't work, and there are too many variables that you won't be able to account for. As we saw with the Six Stages of Personal

Change, when you do finally change some area of your life, it will likely be because you stumbled into the process and met the requirements to move forward. But if we look at Stage Three of the process, we can see that it's all about finding a new path we connect to and deciding to take it. In other words, Stage Three is all about taking the time to figure out what it is you really want.

Saying that you want to change your life, or even saying that you want to change any of the individual parts, is great, but figuring out what it is that you want is how you put a definition to that statement. Clarity is the secret sauce to making your goals real, and it's the number one thing that will enable you to take that critical first step.

HOW TO FIGURE OUT WHAT YOU WANT

As we saw in Stage One of the Six Stages model, when you experience a moment of frustration combined with a moment of inspiration, it creates a unique opportunity for you to start navigating the process of changing your life. We get frustrated and recognize that there must be something better out there, we start searching for and discovering the other options available to us, then we find something that resonates and we start to take action to create that reality. Simple, clean, easy.

In order to figure out what it is you want, you first need to know what your options are. You know what your current situation looks like—that's Option 1. But what else is out there? To find out, you need to start paying attention to the world around you and actively searching for the answer.

Something I've noticed about my own day-to-day behavior is that the areas of my life that I struggle with the most tend to be directly related to the amount of attention I'm exerting in that area. For example, if I'm struggling to pay my bills on time or make more money, it's often because I'm not consciously paying attention to my spending or my income opportunities. Similarly, if I'm struggling to lose those last few stubborn pounds, it's usually because I'm not paying close enough attention to what I'm eating and what I'm getting done at the gym. Maybe this sounds familiar.

When our relationships are suffering, it's often because we aren't giving them the attention they need to thrive. The same can be said for our bodies, our money, our career, and any other area we care about. This concept holds true when it comes to having a clear direction in life. Many— I'd argue most—people don't really know what they want. This isn't surprising considering that we rarely take the time to actually think about that question and explore the potential answers. Have you ever sat down to think about what you want in each individual area of your life? Do you have a specific idea of how you want your body to look and feel? Do you know how much money you want to make? Do you know what your dream relationship looks like? Have you gone through any of the core areas of your life and set a target for what you are trying to accomplish?

Take the time to sit down and come up with those answers. Doing this will give you some early directions to consider. From there, take the time to be exposed to other people and what their lives looks like in the same way that Matt did. It may seem like a lot of work, but try attending networking events, mixers, town events, or conferences in your area to expand your circle of friends. After all, you can't know whether or not something is an option for you if you don't even know that it exists.

Another way to get an idea of what you want your life to look like is to pay attention to things that make you feel jealous or envious, especially on social media. When you are mindlessly scrolling through your Instagram feed and you feel jealous over a photo of someone hiking with their partner, it's a good indication that you perhaps want to go hiking more often, or that you want a partner who enjoys the outdoors, or that you simply want a partner you can do your favorite activities with (even if that doesn't include hiking). Your emotional reactions to the things you see are a good thing to pay attention to when you are trying to determine what it is you want for your own life.

Tiny Leap

When trying to decide what it is you want for your life, it's important to keep your options open to ensure that you are giving yourself the best chance of finding something you truly care about. Paying attention to the things you are jealous of, the things you envy, and the people you look up to can be a great way to identify things that you might want to incorporate into your life.

CHALLENGE

Create a list of ten things you want in your life, and place each of them into one of these five categories:

1. Health
2. Relationships
3. Career
4. Finances
5. Mind-set

Completing this activity will give you a clear understanding of the ambitions that are most important to you.

Once you have a complete list, choose the goals you'd actually be willing to work for. That might sound strange, but very often the goals we set for ourselves don't get accomplished because they aren't things we were ever really willing to work for in the first place. We might want them, but we aren't willing to sacrifice for them, and therefore, we'll never actually accomplish them. An easy way to see what you're willing to work on is to analyze your natural reactions to those goals: Are you going back and forth on what the result should be, or being very general about it? Are you struggling with the idea of executing it?

When you notice resistance toward any of the items on your list, it could be a good indication that you may not actually want or care about that thing. Sure, it'd be nice to have, but it's not a must-have. If it were a must-have, then you would likely have no issue pursuing it. The point of this activity is to recognize that setting a goal is an aspirational action. You are selecting something that you aspire to have in your life. There is no actual action or follow-through required to set a goal. All you need to be able to do is aspire to have something.

HOW TO SET S.M.A.R.T. GOALS

After you've determined what it is you want by strategically setting goals and eliminating the things that don't resonate with you, it's time to double down on the things you do care about and make your goals even better.

A big reason we struggle with achieving a goal is because it's not a good goal to begin with. Sure, the thing you want to accomplish may be great, but if the way you create your goal isn't helping you to actually move toward it, then it's a bad goal. Here's an example of how most people set their goals:

BOB: Hey, Jim, Happy New Year! What's your resolution?

JIM: Hey, Bob! Well, you know, I'd really like to finally get that promotion this year.

BOB: Wow, that sounds great. Best of luck, man!

Every New Year, people have conversations just like this one. In January, we set our resolutions, check in to see how we are doing in February, and the elite among us might even do another check-in in March, but by April, the conversations stop happening, the goal disappears, and we forget that we ever wanted to accomplish it. There are a lot of reasons why this happens every year, but a huge piece of the puzzle is the quality of the goal or resolution that we set for ourselves. Simply put: If we set better goals to begin with, we will naturally achieve more of them.

Going back to the conversation between Jim and Bob,

what exactly was wrong with Jim's goal? Let's take a deeper look.

"I'd really like to finally get that promotion this year." There are a few major issues with this:

1. The goal does not describe a specific action to achieve the desired income.
2. There is no clear time frame to create regular milestones.
3. The goal doesn't provide much context around what is required to accomplish it.
4. There is no direct or indirect method for him to measure his progress.

Unfortunately, this is how many of us set goals. They are well intentioned, and we want them to work, but owing to some fundamental issues, they end up hurting our chances more than helping them. Our goals are often generic, they don't move us to action, and as a result, they don't get done.

So what are the qualities of a good goal? A good goal, one that moves us toward the things we want, is specific, is capable of being measured, drives us to action, is realistic, and has a clear time limit. This is called the S.M.A.R.T. framework, and it's one of the best tools I've found to ensuring my goals are good ones to pursue. Perhaps this isn't the first time you are hearing about the S.M.A.R.T.

framework. That is not a coincidence. Instead of letting your eyes glaze over this section, take the amount you've heard of this framework as reassurance that it *works*.

The origin of the S.M.A.R.T. goal framework isn't known with 100 percent certainty, but it's generally accepted that it was first written down in November 1981 by a gentleman named George T. Doran in his paper titled "There's a S.M.A.R.T. Way to Write Management's Goals and Objectives."[1] George, a consultant at the time, worked with companies to help them improve corporate strategy and goal setting. He believed that the goals his clients were setting were not helping them move forward, so he created the S.M.A.R.T. framework to help them set better ones.

Let's look at the individual pieces:

S: Specific
M: Measurable
A: Assignable
R: Realistic
T: Time-related

Specific

The S in S.M.A.R.T. stands for specific and is essentially a micro-version of the entire concept we are exploring in this chapter. Simply put, if you don't know where you are going, it will be quite difficult to get there. Setting a goal that is specific allows you to chart a map toward it, and can better measure whether or not you've accomplished the goal. It's the difference between saying, "Hey, let's meet at the Starbucks on the corner of Thirty-second and Third," and saying, "Hey, let's meet at Starbucks." If you say the former to someone, they'll know exactly where you are and be able to find you, but if you say the latter, it will take a lot more unnecessary time and energy. This is exactly how your goals work.

Jim's goal from earlier gets an A in specificity. He is clearly stating what he wants to happen. This also has the added bonus of creating the criteria for measuring whether or not he has achieved the goal.

Measurable

I heard a great quote once that went something like "What gets measured grows." Tracking your progress and measuring your success is the number one thing you can do to help start or gain momentum toward the goals you want to accomplish. The process of tracking has many benefits, but chief among them is that it enables you to keep that goal on your mind at all times.

If we think back to the example with Jim, a big part of why his goal was never going to happen is because there was nothing for him to measure or track. This means that eventually, as life got complicated, he was going to forget about working toward a promotion. Keeping your goal on your mind as much as you can is a great hack that will enable you to take more actions toward accomplishment, and it also has the benefit of allowing you to gain satisfaction from the progress you make along the way, which will naturally lead to even more action taken and momentum built.

While Jim's goal was specific, it does not have great measurability. A goal like receiving a promotion has a clear end result that can be tracked. This by itself is good because it allows us to measure success, but success is only a small piece of what needs to be determined. With Jim's goal as it currently is, there is no way to measure progress, because the goal itself is based on a result that he doesn't have complete control over.

Assignable

We set goals because we desire an outcome. A result we desire is somewhere in the distance, and we must move toward it if we want to reach it. A *good* goal's job is to move you toward it. As such, if your goal doesn't have clearly assignable actions involved, then it is not going to serve you when trying to accomplish it.

To create goals that move us toward them, we need to state or imply the action required to make them happen. Jim's goal fails when it comes to being assignable. Sure, he could easily sit down to figure out what actions are required to make the goal happen, but because it states a general desire ("I'd really like...") rather than a course of action, the goal itself is more of a "nice-to-have" instead of a "need-to-have."

When you look at your goal, does it clearly communicate what you need to do? Can you make a list of actions that will move you from Point A to Point B? Are those actions clear? Are the micro-steps required to take each of those actions also clear? Don't be afraid to go deep here: The more you clarify the steps required to accomplish your goals, the higher the chances that you'll actually take those actions and start to make progress on the goals you've set.

Realistic

The goal you set for yourself needs to be realistic in order for you to stay motivated and take consistent action each day. You might be thinking, *What do you mean? If I'm going to set a goal, shouldn't I shoot for the stars?* The short answer to that is no.

The longer answer is that you need to have two separate sets of goals. Your life goal needs to be big and scary and impossible seeming. A big goal is one of the best ways to keep yourself consistently progressing instead of getting complacent. But your other goals, the ones you are actively working to cross off each day, need to feel attainable. You can do this by having a much larger goal and then breaking it down into more realistic pieces or milestones. This will allow you to stay motivated in the long term, because your goal will be worth pursuing, while still being motivated in the short term to take consistent action with the feeling that you can actually achieve your goal.

Jim's goal gets an A here, as it's realistic for most people to achieve a promotion of some kind at their job, especially if they've been there for a significant amount of time.

Time-related

Your goal should have an expiration date. This expiration date serves to keep you focused, helps you take actions daily, and is a constant reminder that you are on a timeline. Without a time limit on our goals, we tend to drag out our work and spend time focusing on far less important things, such as debating minutiae, chasing perfection, and dragging out something that should have taken half the time.

If you want to actually accomplish your goals, then you need to set a very clear deadline, and this will keep your focus where it needs to be, and less on the stuff that doesn't matter. Try setting your due dates in thirty-, sixty-, or ninety-day chunks. Setting a five-year, or even a one-year, goal does you no good because the timeline is so long that it doesn't create that sense of urgency that is necessary to keep you focused.

Unfortunately, Jim's goal has no time limit attached to

it, and there is no realistic way to add one, since landing a promotion is not ultimately within his control. As such, it fails this piece of the puzzle.

Think about the S.M.A.R.T. framework as a step-by-step checklist you can use to set strong goals. Each step is critical, and together, they create the criteria that need to be met in order to have the best chance at accomplishment. If your goals don't meet the criteria, then you need to take a step back and refine them until they do check all the boxes. Using this framework, how could we improve Jim's goal? If you remember, his original goal was the following: *"I'd really like to finally get that promotion this year."*

If we run that goal through our new process, we might come up with something like: *"I want to get a promotion during my annual review this August."* This new goal is better because it states a specific end result, it is framed in a way that enables Jim to take action toward it, and it now has a clear cut-off date that he is working toward. It still doesn't enable him to measure progress easily, but when he sits down to break down action steps, it will get far more measurable than before.

Another way that Jim could dramatically improve his chances of achieving his goal is if he switched his focus completely to something that was more within his control. Instead of setting a goal to achieve a promotion, he could sit down to figure out what actions or results would best position him to negotiate for a promotion during his review. Then he could set a goal of achieving each of those results or actions by the time his review comes.

Tiny Leap

Your ability to achieve your goals is directly related to the quality of goals you set. Utilize the S.M.A.R.T. framework when setting your goals to make them stronger and more actionable to move you forward.

CHALLENGE

Go through the remaining items on your list from the last challenge and review the goals you set based on the framework and process we've just explored. Take some time to analyze each one and make sure you're being S.M.A.R.T. about the actions you'll take to accomplish them.

THE ENDOWMENT EFFECT

After you've identified what you want and set your intentions through action-driven goals, you might not realize the secret psychological effect that comes from combining these two activities. In 1991, psychologist Daniel Kahneman along with economists Jack L. Knetsch and Richard H. Thaler published a paper in the *Journal of Economic Perspectives* titled "Anomalies: The Endowment Effect, Loss Aversion, and Status Quo Bias."[2] In it, they detailed the results of an experiment in which participants were given a mug and the opportunity to trade it for an equally valued object. What they found is that people, once they feel they have ownership over something, will value it at roughly twice the amount they would pay in order to attain it in the first place.

By identifying what you want, and then doing work to improve the quality of your goals around what you want, you are laying the groundwork to feel a sense of ownership over those goals. Sure, you may not yet have the physical manifestation of the thing you want, but you will feel a sense of ownership over the goals themselves. They'll become a part of your identity. Once this happens, you'll be willing to do more to hold on to that idea, and as a result, you'll be far more likely to achieve the goals you've set. Once you truly value the things you have identified as your goal, the endowment effect will do a couple of things for you:

1. Make It Harder Not to Take Action

When you have a sense of ownership over an identity that is tied directly to your goals, it makes it difficult not to act in accordance. We humans have a shockingly accurate ability to take actions that align with the way we identify ourselves, and it's no different here. If the goals you set are a part of your identity, you'll be more likely to do the things required to pursue that goal.

2. Make It Easier to Deal with Failure

When you are pursuing your goals, there is always going to be the experience of failure. No one is capable of achieving *everything* they set out to do, but failure will become much easier to deal with because you'll be acting in accordance with the goals you have ownership over. That sense of identity will give us a reason to push through when things are difficult.

Now you know it's incredibly important to understand what you want and to set action-driving goals to move you toward them, but none of that matters if you don't have a strong reason for the things you want in the first place. And the most interesting part of this is that a strong *why* is probably even more important than the how.

CHAPTER THREE

THE IMPORTANCE OF WHY

He who has a why to live for can bear almost any
how.   —*Friedrich Nietzsche*

"Why is Apple so innovative?"

This is one of the first questions Simon Sinek, the *New York Times*–bestselling author of *Start with Why*, asks in his wildly popular TED talk titled "How Great Leaders Inspire Action."[1] This question, as simple as it may seem, led Simon to theorize the reasons why some companies, and some people, seem to be able to move others to action, whether that action is buying a product or working harder, while the vast majority of companies and people are not able to do that.

He called this theory the "Golden Circle" and it lays out the foundation for a "Why"-centered approach to business—one that many around the world have adopted into their daily behavior. In his words: "People don't buy what you do, they buy why you do it."

When Apple first opened their doors on April 1, 1976, Steve Jobs and Steve Wozniak had a clear "Why" behind their product. After spending much of their time toying with the MITS Altair 8800 computer at their local computer club, they decided to create something that was easier to use for the average person. Forty-two years later, this core "Why" can still be seen in Apple's commitment to creating technology that doesn't feel like technology.

Based on Simon's theory, if you want to inspire someone to take action on your behalf, you first need to understand and communicate your reasoning. But before you can convince other people of doing things, you need to convince yourself, right? Luckily, the same principle holds true when trying to inspire yourself to take action.

One of the main reasons people don't accomplish the things they'd like to, or even come close, is because we lose the initial excitement and momentum that drove us to set the goal in the first place. We go through Stages One and Two. We get fired up after a moment of frustration, and we become singularly focused on changing our life, but then we get stuck in the second stage because it takes a while to find an option that resonates. The more time passes between the initial motivation and the decision, the less likely it is that we will move forward.

Think about your New Year's resolutions from last year. If you're like most Americans, you probably went through the following cycle:

1. Excitement for the new year and it's seemingly endless potential to reset and take control of your life
2. Motivation during the first few days of exploring new options or even execution
3. Realization of how difficult sticking with it actually is
4. Frustration and eventually lack of interest as you fall back into existing habits

Does that process sound familiar? It's not just about New Year's resolutions either—all of our unaccomplished goals tend to follow a similar pattern. Setting and then subsequently dropping New Year's resolutions is a pastime around the world. On the surface, this could be a good thing. After all, if we are setting resolutions every year, it means that there is a moment in time each year when people wake up and try to start living their life consciously rather than walking through it in a zombie-like haze.

When we dive deeper, though, New Year's resolutions might be doing more damage than good. After failing at accomplishing their resolutions for a few years in a row, some people make the unfortunate decision to stop consciously setting goals altogether because it seems, in the short term, easier not to set any goals rather than fail, and deal with the frustration. It's an unfortunate decision that keeps them trapped in a cycle. Setting goals isn't the real issue that needs to be addressed—the problem lies in the reason behind our goals.

Again, if you are like most people, you probably create your New Year's resolutions as a part of the annual ritual. That's not to say you don't want to accomplish these goals, but by doing it because you "feel like you should" or "everyone else is doing it," you are not emotionally connecting. This is why taking the time to figure out your *why* is an important step.

It might seem difficult to find a why, especially one that seems worth pursuing, but the benefits of having one are real. Your why is the thing that stops you from quitting when things get tough and you just want to throw in the towel. It's what drives you to move forward when you experience failure after failure with no chance of success in sight. Your why is the engine behind the day-to-day actions you'll need to take in order to create real change in the long term.

Let's look at an example of how this might play out in practice: Dave has a goal to increase his income by 50 percent over the next three years. His why for this goal is that he wants his daughter to graduate from college debt-free (or with very little debt) and start her adult life farther ahead than he did. To make this happen, he's decided ahead of time to do a few things:

1. Get consecutive raises at work at each annual review
2. Start a side business
3. Create a separate savings account
4. Set up automatic transfers that come out of his account before he sees them

That's a very basic strategy, right? But executing this plan will result in the successful completion of the goal.

When you really break it down, the required steps to accomplishing any goal are usually pretty simple and straightforward. We are logical creatures and can reason out the steps required to make something happen. So why don't most of us achieve more of our goals? There are two challenges we face:

1. Getting started on our goals after we've identified the steps
2. Building momentum to keep us going until the actions become normal

Luckily, finding a strong why can help us navigate these pitfalls quite well, but let's dive deeper into these two factors to explore why they affect us so much and how we should be thinking about them.

WHY WE STRUGGLE WITH GETTING STARTED

Did you know that when you try to move any object, it requires more force to get it moving than it will require to keep it going? This happens because of two physical forces called static friction, the force that keeps a stationary object at rest, and kinetic friction, the force that brings it to a stop once it's moving. In general, static friction is greater than kinetic friction, which is why it requires more force up front to get a stationary object moving than it requires to keep it moving.

Have you ever noticed how difficult it is to get started on something? How, no matter how badly you might want it, it feels impossible to get moving? But then once you do start, it suddenly feels easier and easier to keep things moving in the right direction and progressing?

Like all other objects in the world, we're experiencing static friction *pushing* against us whenever we consider starting. All the small things in our day-to-day life contribute to making it more difficult. Maybe we don't feel like we have enough time, maybe our kids are demanding, maybe we are just overwhelmed constantly. Whatever it is that is holding us back can be considered a form of static friction doing its job and keeping us in one place. Once we manage to overcome that force, however, using whatever means necessary, it takes far less energy for us to keep things going than it did for us to start.

Taking action toward the goals you've set will be much easier if you realize the biggest commitment of energy will need to be in the beginning of virtually everything you do, whether it's learning a new language, getting yourself to the gym, or starting up a business. Eventually, the new activity will become one of habit and will be far easier to maintain than it was to get started.

HOW TO KEEP THINGS GOING ONCE YOU'VE STARTED

So you've managed to get started, but that doesn't mean you can just slack off. Success, after all, requires a disciplined pursuit of progress every single day. Thankfully, when you start something, you are far more likely to return to it at a later time. This is called the *Ovsiankina effect*.[2] Theorized by psychologist Maria Ovsiankina, the effect states that humans have a tendency to pick up an interrupted action again when it has still not been achieved. The act of starting something, and not achieving it, causes us to consistently think about that thing and the fact that it was never completed. It becomes a "quasi-need," a short-term need based not on anything we actually require for survival, but instead on the situation you find yourself in. For example, if you are caught in the rain, you feel like you need an umbrella or a raincoat. That need isn't biological, but it is strong enough to cause you to take action in a similar way that a biological need to eat would. Being conscious of the Ovsiankina effect can do wonders for you when trying to accomplish a goal because it allows you to, once started, feel as though you need to return to the goal and see it through to completion.

Building Habits

You've probably heard somewhere that it takes twenty-one days of repetition for a new habit to be formed. This is correct to an extent but it leaves out some important information. Forming habits is a complicated matter, and it requires a different amount of time for each person, each habit, and each situation.

With that said, here's a good rule of thumb: Do something consistently every day for three months and it will become difficult not to do that thing. That doesn't necessarily mean that it's a habit (it might take up to an entire year to make something complicated into a habit), but you'll be more likely to keep it going each day, and ultimately, that's what matters. Giving yourself the opportunity to create habits that reinforce your specific goal will go a long way toward helping you accomplish it. But in order to create a habit, the circumstances need to be more or less the same each time.

Here's what I mean: Let's say that you want to build a habit of flossing every day. On the first day, you floss after brushing in the morning, on the second you floss at night, and on the third you floss after your last meal. In the short term, this is great—you are accomplishing your goal and flossing each day, which is what ultimately matters. You continue that process for three months, and each day you floss at a different time. You get it done, but it's tough to remember. After three months, you've flossed every single day. That's a huge accomplishment and you should celebrate.

But over that time, you've missed out on a pretty huge opportunity. You may have flossed every day, but you never developed any routines around it, and without those, it becomes more difficult for a habit to be formed. If you had decided ahead of time that you would floss every morning after brushing your teeth and stuck with it, after three months you'd find that it had become a natural behavior. In fact, it would become just as natural as brushing your teeth.

This is called *habit stacking*, and it's an incredibly effective approach to creating new habits and routines. Habit stacking is the act of introducing a new activity within the context of an existing routine, making it easier to do in the long term, thus creating a habit.

In the first example, you accomplished your goal each day, but you didn't lay any groundwork that would help you reduce the static friction you needed to overcome to accomplish the goal, so each day would be just as hard as the last, and perhaps more important, it would always be easier for you to drop the activity as soon as things got tough rather than keeping the activity going.

Tiny Leap

Turning the actions you need to take regularly into habits is the best way to ensure that you consistently do them. When first starting out, try doing the activity immediately after something else that is already a habit. By stacking it on top of an existing habit, you'll make it easier for the activity to turn into a routine.

Now that we understand what is involved in both getting started on a goal and keeping it going for the long haul, let's do a quick review of Dave's goal:

GOAL: To increase his income by 50 percent over the next three years.

WHY: So that his daughter can graduate from college debt-free (or with very little debt) and start her adult life farther ahead than he did.

Let's assume that Dave gets started on his goal immediately, putting in more effort at work and making sure he stands out. He also spends a few weeks taking the time to audit the skills he has and eventually finds a service that he can build a side hustle around. Dave is off to a great start! He made a decision and then used the excitement he felt to catapult himself forward.

Here's when it might get hard: Six months in, someone on his team at work gets promoted over him for a job he was hoping to land. It's frustrating—Dave has been working his tail off. He's crushed every single task assigned to him. He's consistently brought new ideas to the table and always gets great feedback from his manager. He knows that he's more qualified than the person who actually got the promotion. However, when he asks his boss why he wasn't considered for the position, she says that the other person just had more leadership experience than he did.

On top of all of that, the last three months have been hectic and full of late nights at the office because of a big project. Dave hasn't had a good night's sleep in two months because he still has to get client projects finished, even if that means coming home late.

To make matters worse, Dave has been fighting with his wife more often. Not about anything important, just little things here and there that he usually would have more patience for. He knows that it's his fault because he can clearly feel the effects of his lack of sleep and is noticeably more irritable than usual and constantly on edge.

This all may sound extreme, but it's a natural side effect of aiming to do more or something bigger. When you set out to make a change, you'll need to get it done while still maintaining the other areas of your life. Often people find themselves overwhelmed, stressed, fatigued, and ready to fight at all times. Not because they are bad people, but because change, by definition, requires going above and beyond what you are accustomed to handling.

If Dave experiences something like this, he'll see his output at work start to decline. He'll notice himself stop pushing for new clients with his side business. He'll wake up one day burned out and exhausted. Then, before he realizes it, he'll slip back into his prior day-to-day behavior, allowing the goal to go out of focus and become a distant memory.

This kind of thing happens all the time. It's probably a pattern you've experienced when trying to pursue a challenging goal—things start out strong, your enthusiasm increases, and you make some progress. Then life starts to get difficult, as it often does, and it creates a cycle of frustration that either throws you off your path completely or causes so much turmoil in the rest of your life that you end up having to choose between progress toward your goal or maintaining personal balance.

In order for a diamond to be created, carbon must

undergo intense pressure and heat for an extended period of time. So you, too, must undergo intense pressure when trying to make a change in your life or accomplish a goal. But dealing with pressure isn't easy—often it just causes you to fall back into old behaviors, often the habits and routines that you've already developed over your life. And life doesn't care whether or not those easy behaviors come at the expense of the future you want.

So how do you and Dave deal with it when you are trying to make progress and life decides to throw everything but the kitchen sink directly at your face? The easiest thing you can do when trying to challenge this cycle is to have a strong why behind your goals. If you want to go even further, have a why that you are forcibly reminded of every single day.

In Dave's example, the minute that life decides to punch him in the face, there's a much higher chance that he'll be able to pull himself together and slowly work through the frustrations and issues that he experiences because his why is his daughter's success. After all, what's his alternative? He has to wake up every day and look in his daughter's face. He is constantly reminded of the two potential outcomes for her life, both of which he is in complete control of. If he decides to let life beat him and cripple his ability to make progress, he is virtually assuring that his daughter will have a harder time going to a good school and graduating without putting herself too far into a hole of debt.

On a day-to-day basis, some changes would need to be made in order for Dave to adapt to these frustrations without sacrificing his relationships or quality of life, but the moment he felt like quitting, or the moment that his behavior started to slide back into its old norms, he'd see his daughter and instantly be reminded of the future he is trying to create for her.

Picture yourself in Dave's situation. Which path would you take if you were constantly forced to remember the reason behind why you are working hard and sacrificing in the short term? I'm guessing that you'd probably try to do everything in your power to keep things moving regardless of what life might throw at you. Having a strong why for your goals works because it allows you to re-sell yourself on the idea when you start to lose interest. It allows you to get your emotions involved and to re-create that initial spark of excitement that drove your decision to take action in the first place.

Tiny Leap

Your why needs to be easy to remember. Try writing it down on a few Post-it Notes and posting them in your most heavily trafficked areas such as your car, desk, the refrigerator door, or the back of your bedroom door.

A strong why is like a shot of motivation that can be applied in those moments when you need it most. It's like a superpower to get yourself to keep going no matter how tough or frustrating life is getting. Figuring out your why is one of the best things you can do when trying to change your life, and even though it might be difficult, it's probably the worthiest use of your time at any given moment. Even more, it allows you the opportunity to pull on that why for motivation when you most need it. So how do you go about finding it?

HOW TO FIND YOUR WHY

Finding your why might be the hardest part of this whole process to navigate because we often don't exactly recognize the subconscious reasons for wanting to change our life. Your why is going to be something very personal to you—in fact, it has to be. A personal why is the only thing that can really drive you forward when things get tough, so take the time required to find a why that really matters to you.

As an example, plenty of people say that they want to get rich. When asked why, they may say things like, "I want to live in a nice house" or "I want to retire early and travel" or "Life is easier when you have money." Saying that you want to be rich because of any of those reasons is fine, but that's usually not the root cause of the desire to make a lot of money. If they were willing to dig deeper, they might realize that they want to live in a nice house because they want their family to be proud of them, or maybe they want to retire early and travel because they've never had the opportunity to leave their hometown, or perhaps they think life will be easier because a lack of money causes them a lot of stress.

Regardless of what the true why behind a goal is, the more you allow yourself to drill down to its roots and identify the core of it, the more you'll start to feel an emotional attachment. Don't get confused about what role your why needs to play in your life. It does not need to be some deep, meaningful thing that can surface only through years of therapy. Your why could simply be that you want to avoid the stress of not having enough money. In fact, that's the reason that most people stay at jobs they may not like all that much. They need the money, and so they keep going in each day. It's that simple.

A why doesn't need to be meaningful or deep, but it does need to be relevant and emotionally important to you. Otherwise, it won't be able to serve you when you find yourself ready to quit. Here is a brief list of criteria that you should try to execute to ensure you have a strong why:

1. Your why should be personal.
2. Your why should carry emotional weight.
3. Your why should be easy to reinforce.

Your Why Should Be Personal

The whole point of figuring out your why is so it can help push you through the struggles that you will inevitably face on your journey. It's meant to be the fuel you need when things get tough and the driving force behind all the decisions you make. A strong why works because it means something to you. It's a part of who you are and, as such, is impossible to forget or ignore.

Think about it: If your goal is to do something relatively difficult like learn how to code and become a software developer, your journey is going to be riddled with frustration and disappointment. You might struggle to find the time necessary to study or complete your projects. Maybe it will be hard to keep things in perspective as you try to get over the learning curve that comes with learning to code. While you navigate this process, if your reason for doing so is just that you want to make more money, you might find it difficult to keep going and easy to say, "Well, I'm just not good enough to code anyway," or "This is too hard; I'm just not wired for it."

Trust me, the above scenario is one I've found myself in

many times. I've tried and failed at becoming a software developer at least five times. Why? My reason for doing it wasn't strong enough. I don't love writing code. I'm not passionate about it. And it never felt like an absolutely necessary career move. The only reason I wanted to do it was because I saw how much software developers could get paid, and I have an enormous amount of student loan debt.

But let's contrast that with learning to produce and distribute audio, video, and written content. There are enormous learning curves when it comes to content production. You need to learn how to edit, you need to learn the best practices, you need to learn how to record the raw content, and so on. The learning curve is just as steep as learning to code and it pulls on far more diverse skills, yet I've gotten quite good at each of these elements and have managed to shape them into my career. So why didn't I get stuck on this learning curve just as I did with becoming a software developer?

Well, I knew from the moment I first started learning media production that it was something I needed to do. Not only was the process fun, but there was a unique sense of satisfaction that came from being able to dream something up and actually get it out into the world, which drove me to take any class I could on the subject and consistently spend time either learning more about it or actively doing it. Whenever I'd hit a wall and get frustrated, I would naturally return to it because it was something I enjoyed.

Simply put, my why for learning media production was because I *loved* it. That strong, personal why allowed me to keep going when things got tough and pushed me forward no matter what happened. You have that same potential—you simply need to dig deep and find a why that matters to you and your life. Do that and you'll find it easier than ever to accomplish your goals.

Your Why Should Carry Emotional Weight

According to Freud's psychoanalytic theory of personality, the Pleasure Principle[3] describes the human tendency to seek pleasure and avoid pain. Tony Robbins further developed this idea for the purposes of behavioral modification, and the core of his idea is summarized by his quote, "People will do more to avoid pain than they will do to gain pleasure." To combine these ideas, humans tend to naturally seek pleasure and avoid pain, but it's not an equal relationship. Our tendency to avoid pain outweighs our desire to pursue pleasure, which creates an imbalance between the two ideas that many a salesperson has taken advantage of to make a sale. In fact, one of the first things you learn about sales or marketing is that people respond better when you speak to their pain points: When something is presented as a solution to pain, especially the extreme kind, it becomes a "must-have." When something is presented as a bonus, it becomes a "nice-to-have."

So what does a sales technique have to do with finding your why? The Pleasure Principle isn't just a sales technique. It's a method of motivation that, if utilized well, can drive people to take actions in their favor. When we view this idea in the context of choosing a why that carries emotional weight, the pleasure we are seeking and the pain we are avoiding can be seen as the emotional weight attached to a particular why. If we identify a why that is personal to us, and one in which failure creates pain and success creates pleasure, then we are more likely to progress toward our goals.

Let's look at Dave's goal again—to increase his income and save the majority of it so that his daughter could graduate from college debt-free. This is both a personal goal and one that carries some serious emotional weight. Failure at accomplishing his goal could mean letting his daughter down, compromising her future, and perhaps lowering his self-esteem.

Does that mean that it's impossible for him to fail because he has a good goal with a lot of emotional weight?

Of course not. But if people are willing to do more to move away from pain than they are to gain pleasure, such a personal goal will make it much more difficult for Dave to pack up and quit just because things get difficult. The

Pleasure Principle is a powerful tool in your arsenal, but it can be utilized only if you are willing to find a why that has significant emotional weight attached to both success and failure.

Your Why Should Be Easy to Reinforce

Scientists working at the University of Basel in Switzerland published a study in the journal *Cell* in 2014 that begins its summary with, "A plastic nervous system requires the ability not only to acquire and store but also to forget."[4] The study found, as you can probably guess, that in order to remain efficient at day-to-day tasks, the brain actively scrubs itself of what it considers to be "superfluous" information.

What do you think are the chances that your unaccomplished goals might fall under the "superfluous" category? My guess is that they're pretty high. Much of what the brain considers important to keep is related to the things you experience on a day-to-day basis. This is part of the reason it's so much easier to focus on getting through our routine rather than moving ourselves forward. Your why needs to be on your mind as often as possible, and this will allow your brain to recognize that it is important to keep around, thus avoiding the "superfluous" trap.

Let's look at Dave's goal one more time. Let's say that

things have gotten tough. He and his wife are fighting constantly, he has no time for sleep, and he isn't making progress as quickly as he was hoping. What do you think Dave would do if he considered quitting his plan and then, as soon as he got home from work, his daughter ran up to him and gave him a big hug? Assuming Dave is a human, his heart would probably melt immediately and it would renew his willingness to push through.

Now let's take a look at my goal of becoming a software developer. If you remember, my reason for doing it was simply that I wanted to make more money and get out of debt. You might think that would be a why with emotional weight attached to it, but it wasn't something I connected with on a day-to-day basis. Sure, it's no fun making my payments each month, but outside of that single period of time when I'm reminded of how frustrated I am, my life is more or less unaffected. In other words, there aren't enough reminders in place that I have to confront. All this together leads to an easily forgettable why that doesn't lend itself to pushing through tough times.

Finding a why that you're easily reminded of is important. Our lives are busy and we have an endless number of things to consider each and every day—our brains just aren't capable of or willing to store all that information forever.

Tiny Leap

If something isn't at the forefront of our thoughts, it often isn't on our minds at all. Find a why that can be reinforced easily through constant or regular exposure so that when things get tough and you need motivation the most, it will always be on your mind.

CHALLENGE

Pick one of your goals and identify a strong why for pursuing it. Ensure that your why matches the criteria we've discussed in this chapter:

1. It must be personal.
2. It must have emotional weight.
3. It must be easily reinforced.

CHAPTER FOUR

AUDIT YOUR REALITY

I think, to me, reality is better than being fake.

—*Ice Cube*

Julia Calder spent New Year's Eve 2016 like many other twenty-somethings: eating too little food and drinking too much alcohol.

She was out with friends celebrating, and from the outside looking in, she seemed to be having a great time. That is, until she blacked out.

Julia's friend, who was leading a paint night event at the bar they were visiting, asked Julia, who'd had a few too many drinks, to keep an eye on the painting she had just spent hours working on while she ran to the restroom. While she was gone, Julia took a brush, dipped it into jet-black paint, and smeared it over the surface of her friend's work. Later that night, Julia found herself in her apartment with a strange man standing behind her. It was her Uber driver. She doesn't remember if she invited him in or if he followed her, but she does recall the intense fear she felt in that moment. Thankfully, when he was asked to leave, the driver departed with no issues.

The next morning, when asked why she had painted over her friend's artwork, she had no memory of it. She was also well aware of how badly having a stranger in her apartment could have turned out. Julia realized that the direction her life was going was not where she wanted it to go. If she continued living the way she was, things might end up much worse the next time she drank. What Julia unknowingly did that morning was take a quick, but effective, audit of her behavior and compared it to the life she knew she wanted for herself.

When she realized that they didn't match up, she made a change and started over.

Once we've identified what it is that we want, we should audit our behaviors and our reality regularly in order to gauge how they hold up against the goal. This process of reflection is what allows us to move forward. It gives us ammunition to use against ourselves. Reflection allows us to get a real, in-our-face view of our performance and gives us a metric with which we can compare our lives to our ideal. It provides much-needed context—the kind that most of us don't have—around our day-to-day behavior and gives us information that we can work with.

Back in 2016, I quit my full-time job and started free-lancing as a web designer and podcast consultant. At the beginning of each month, I found myself struggling to make ends meet. I never had enough revenue coming in, I could never put aside savings, and I certainly couldn't even begin to think about growing my business. I fell into a cycle that repeated itself every single month, and yet every single month I was shocked. I had all the skills, I offered a high-demand service and was very good at it, and I had a network that should have allowed me to succeed. But I didn't.

By the end of 2016, I had run out of money, burned some relationships, and had to take the first job offered to me. What happened?

Well, if you had asked me on any day that year how hard I had worked and where I had spent my time, I probably would have told you that I hustled for thirteen hours a day and was incredibly productive. So then why didn't it work out for me? Well, because I didn't *actually* hustle for thirteen hours and I wasn't all that productive.

Sure, I thought I was working hard all day. I was in front of my computer for hours at a time—that must have meant I was being productive, right? But there's often a huge difference between what we think, or what we remember, and the reality. Had I taken the time to sit down at any point during that year and perform an honest, open, audit on my daily behaviors, I would have seen that I had spent closer to three hours per day actually working, and that those three hours weren't dedicated to my most important tasks. Between getting distracted, switching back and forth between tasks, and just watching videos on YouTube, I was left with a small amount of actual work. Realizing this earlier in the year could have allowed me to change my behavior while I still had time to recover and jump out of the hole I was digging.

But I never performed that audit. Had I known what my behaviors actually were and what patterns existed, I could have made a plan to stay extra focused for a period each day and then spent the rest of the time doing whatever I wanted. Instead, since I wasn't conscious of my behaviors and didn't really know where my time was going, I threw those hours away believing they were necessary to move me forward.

If we have a goal but aren't constantly auditing our behaviors as they relate to that goal, it's shockingly easy to convince ourselves that we are making progress and, as in my case, it's only after we've dug ourselves too deep that we realize it.

WHY WE DON'T PERFORM LIFE AUDITS

If performing a life audit is such an incredible tool for helping us accomplish our goals, why don't we audit our behaviors more often?

There are two main reasons:

1. Cognitive dissonance
2. Confirmation bias

Cognitive Dissonance

Auditing our behaviors can often show us that the way we *think* we act is very different from the reality. That can be very painful to understand. As I said earlier, it's easy to convince ourselves that we are moving in the right direction and taking actions toward what we want, but it's also incredibly easy to convince ourselves that we deserve something because we've worked hard for it.

We've all had this experience or one that is similar: We go to the gym, work out hard, and then have a salad for lunch. Then we take a few rest days. In our minds, we just went to the gym and we ate pretty healthy, but in reality, a week or two have passed and we've started to slip back into old eating habits. Because it's a gradual shift back into something that has been normal, we don't notice it happening. If someone were to ask us, we'd say that we go to the gym and we eat healthy. That's the version of ourselves that we created in our minds by taking part in that activity. But if we sat down and audited our reality and were forced to confront it, that "identity" we've created might be shattered and we'd have a hard time accepting it.

This shattering causes cognitive dissonance[1] to occur. Essentially, as it relates to this scenario, cognitive dissonance is when we hold on to one belief about who we are and what we are doing, while being confronted with another belief that contradicts it. To get a better idea of how this may come into play, think about the last time you did something a little risky that goes against the "type" of person you are. Maybe you took home some office supplies from work, or maybe you accidentally skipped out on a bill at your favorite bar, or maybe you caught yourself flirting a little with that cute guy you bumped into. Regardless of what it was, you aren't the type of person that usually does that, right? But you did. The discomfort you felt when you took a risk was caused by cognitive dissonance.

When experiencing this, people tend to get defensive. Ultimately, we believe that we are good people with good traits. We want to act in accordance with the thing we said we were going to do, or the type of person we believe we are. When we don't and have to face that reality, we get defensive to try and hold on to the original belief.

Bumping up against a reality that contradicts the idea we want to believe can often feel like what Neo experienced after being unplugged from the Matrix. It's a shock to confront a reality you don't want in the face, and as a result, many people choose to take the blue pill and run away from it instead. The problem is that, like most things in life, running away from it doesn't do anything to resolve the issue and this is why, even though it's painful, you need to start taking the time to perform a life audit and confront your reality.

Confirmation Bias

Owing to a phenomenon called confirmation bias,[2] we tend to filter out information that goes against what we already, or want to, believe. In other words, if we think we are working hard toward our goals, we have a built-in tendency to only notice and remember things that "prove" our hard work, while ignoring all the behaviors that contradict it. There are a few leading hypotheses as to why we do this. One hypothesis includes something called the availability heuristic, which has wide-ranging effects on our ability to recall our own positive or negative behavior. When the availability heuristic is a factor, we place trust in the piece of information that most readily comes to mind, even if there's no concrete reason behind it.

Here's an example of how it works: Let's say you have a goal to save more money each month. You've identified your target and even created a clear plan for executing it. If, throughout this process, you believe you are doing a good job and saving money effectively, you'll only pay attention to your behaviors like refusing to go out with friends, or cutting back on groceries, or packing a lunch every day and think, "Wow, I'm really doing a great job with this goal!" All the while you're ignoring random unnecessary purchases, ATM withdrawals, and your refusal to open a savings account.

In my case, when I was freelancing full-time, I believed I was working hard and found examples of that being true while completely ignoring the massive amount of time being wasted each day. In this way, we are always presenting ourselves in the best light when we self-evaluate, and each day is spent finding evidence that we are doing better than we actually are.

While confirmation bias and cognitive dissonance are powerful foes to overcome when trying to change your life, they are not impossible to beat. Auditing your reality regularly will become a habitual activity, which, as you know, will make it easier to do every time. Here, you'll identify potentially dangerous habits or behaviors before they completely derail you on your journey, and you can correct your actions to make regular progress. Facing reality can be painful, but it's a short-term pain that will eventually allow you to achieve more of your goals and improve the overall quality of your life.

Tony Robbins's quote from earlier in this chapter is more important here than ever: "People will do more to avoid pain than they will do to gain pleasure." Yes, the short-term pain of facing reality and your desire to avoid it can be enough to stop you in your tracks and kill any potential action you might take, but auditing your life will give you more pleasure than you can imagine in time. Keep this idea in mind as you follow the path ahead of you. Unplugging the Matrix is painful and may result in disorientation, but it's the only way to make real progress.

Tiny Leap

One easy way to start auditing your behavior is to buy a small notebook and carry it around with you. Each time you engage in a behavior that is either positive or negative toward your end goal, make a note of it. At the end of the day, compare the log to see what percentage of activity was positive and what percentage was negative.

HOW TO AUDIT YOUR REALITY

The secret to successfully auditing your reality comes in the combination of two key habits:

1. Data collection and measurement
2. Metrics-driven reviews

Data Collection and Measurement

The first step is to develop a habit of recording everything as it happens. The goal here is simply to get data collected because as long as it's been recorded somewhere, you'll be able to go back and review it, which is the second piece of this puzzle that we'll discuss in a bit.

Before we continue, I do want to take a moment to say that you shouldn't sit down to record things at the end of the day unless absolutely necessary. If you try to do this, you'll find that your memory of the day is going to be quite flawed, thanks to both confirmation bias and cognitive dissonance. You'll essentially edit your memory of the day to make it seem better than it was. Recording something the minute it happens will allow you to get the most objective understanding. Here are a few ways you can go about data collection:

The Notebook

The easiest approach you can take is to simply carry a pen and a small notebook around with you whenever possible. This may be a fairly analog and old school approach, but it does allow you to whip out the book in the exact moment you need it and write down your activity as soon as it happens.

As an alternative here, you can also keep notes in your phone or in a dedicated note app such as Evernote. Writing down your activity as it happens is an excellent way to record activity around multiple types of goals. If you care most about your fitness, then simply write down all of your activities for the day such as the walks you take or time spent at the gym. If your goal is to procrastinate less, then keep a record of the time you spend working productively for the day. The goal with this system is to create a log of your activity that is relevant to your goal. By doing so, you'll be able to get a factual understanding of how much time is actually being spent in that area and you'll be able to adjust accordingly.

The Apps

The second approach to collecting data is using one of the many apps or wearable technologies that are designed specifically for this purpose.

Mint, a financial management app owned by Intuit, is an excellent recording tool for your budget, spending, and credit information. It connects to all of your bank accounts and keeps track of every bit of income or every expense made. You can then go back in to categorize the transactions and view trend data.

Fitbit is the world leader in fitness recording that allows you to get an accurate understanding of how you are sleeping, how many steps you've taken, and how much activity you've engaged in throughout the day.

MyFitnessPal is the top app for recording your calories, nutrients, and overall food consumption. By entering in your meals, you can also get an understanding of how you are performing in relation to the nutrition goals you've set for yourself.

RescueTime is an app on your computer that helps you better understand the time you've spent on superfluous tasks such as reading random list articles on *BuzzFeed* versus the time you've spent on productive tasks. It does this automatically by running in the background and keeping track of all open applications.

There are many other tools like the four I've just named—in fact, there is an entire industry for wearable devices dedicated to tracking your life. The main drawback with this approach is that it's impossible to accurately categorize every single detail automatically. For example, tools like Mint may be able to catch all of your transactions but it still requires you to go in and ensure that each transaction is categorized properly. If you choose to go the tech route, you'll need to double-check things as much as you can.

But none of this matters without the next piece of the puzzle. Once you've developed a reliable system for collecting information, you need to create a process for reviewing that information regularly.

Metrics-Driven Reviews

Data collection is pointless if you never look at it. How will you know what to change if you don't face the reality of things? To do this effectively and get the most out of this system, you'll need to set aside a dedicated window to comb through your records and review the data. Make sure you plan to do this ahead of time; otherwise your data will simply sit there waiting to help you change your life.

So let's get into the how. To create a metrics-driven review process, you need to do the following:

1. Select a consistent day and time to review your data.
2. Identify which points of data are most important.
3. Compare this key data to performance from your last review.
4. Create a plan for reducing the frequency of "bad" behavior.

We've already covered the importance of the first step, but by dedicating a few hours on a specific day to reflect on the data you've collected, you'll significantly increase the likelihood of actually sitting down to do it. Additionally, by making a set plan to do something, you create a positive confirmation bias toward actually doing it—you are more likely to act in accordance with what you've claimed you'd do, rather than against it. This is why good salespeople try to get you to verbally agree that you need a solution for a problem that their product will fix. It makes it more likely that you'll buy it. You can add psychological pressure to yourself by telling someone else that you'll be reviewing at that time on that day, which will add the element of another person's judgment to the picture, giving you another reason to follow through.

When it's time for you to actually sit down and get the job done, you'll need to know where to focus your efforts. In statistics, there is a concept called the influential point. This means that when trying to find the value of a slope, there can often be a point in the line that breaks away from the pattern, causing you to get a skewed result in value. When tracking your data, you need to find any influential points that might affect your results—these are the areas that truly matter for achieving your goal. For example, if you're trying to save money, you should focus on finding the areas that are costing you the most. If you are trying to be more productive, you need to better understand what factors cause you to procrastinate. Once you've found them, you can make a plan based on doing better in those areas.

Essentially, your goal is to identify the most important pieces of the puzzle so that you can focus on evaluating the performance of these areas. Finally, when the time comes, you need to sit down and complete an honest review with absolutely no judgment. Adding emotions to the situation and beating yourself up will only cause you to alter your own results. Instead, if you keep in mind the goal of improvement rather than judgment, you'll allow yourself to truly understand your behavior.

The first time you review, you'll want to focus on making note of your performance in the influential point areas. The second time around, you'll be able to compare your performance data to previous weeks, so you simply need to create a plan for improving on the numbers by your next review. By tracking the data, you'll automatically start to see changes based simply on being more aware of what your behaviors look like.

Remember Julia from the beginning of this chapter? The process we've just outlined is exactly what Julia had to navigate that morning when she woke up. She was forced to face a shocking reality that contradicted the idea she had of herself. She could see with stunning clarity that if she continued down the path she was heading, something bad would happen to her or someone she cared about.

Over the next few days, Julia silently took stock of her behavior. She didn't change anything immediately, and she certainly wasn't consciously doing it, but she was quietly observing and building a clear picture of the reality she was living in. This period of reflection and acceptance helped dramatically. Today Julia is completely sober, eating healthier than ever, and is building a business of her own that she wants to use to impact others around her. It doesn't feel good to face reality, but if you can better understand the consequences of not changing and create a clear process for making it happen, you'll be far more willing and able to deal with the short-term pain of auditing your reality to avoid the much larger, and longer-term, pain of never becoming the person you so desperately want to be.

Remember, the purpose of this process is not to start changing your life or accomplishing your goals. The purpose is simply to collect the data required to gain an accurate understanding of where you currently are in relationship to those goals.

Tiny Leap

Building the life you want requires changing your day-to-day behavior. To do this, you must first understand what your day-to-day behavior actually looks like and be willing to confront that new reality despite the pain it may cause.

CHALLENGE

Select one of the goals you have for your life and spend a single day auditing your reality as it relates to that area. Use the process outlined in this chapter to track your behavior and then perform an audit based on the metrics-driven review system.

CHAPTER FIVE

CHANGE YOUR BEHAVIOR

Action is the foundational key to all success.

—*Pablo Picasso*

Tal Gur had recently finished grad school when he found himself sitting in a room, surrounded by friends, and unsure of what to do next. At thirty years old, he had devoted the majority of his life so far to the educational process, but now that he was finished, it wasn't clear what he should do with his time and his life overall. After a conversation with his friends about achieving bucket list items, inspiration struck: Tal decided to create a list of a hundred life goals that he wanted to accomplish. These weren't easy goals either—these were incredible bucket list items that many dream of accomplishing at some point in their life.

You might be thinking, "Why does it matter that this

random person created a bucket list?" After all, most of us have some kind of dream goal that we want to accomplish. The amazing thing about Tal is that, after sitting down at the age of thirty and creating a hundred goals that he wanted to accomplish, he actually set out and accomplished them. That's right, every single one of the goals were completed over ten years. A *hundred* life goals in *ten* years. It's the basis for his book, *The Art of Fully Living*, and as I've said, they were not easy. Just a few of the items on his list included:

- Finishing a full Ironman triathlon
- Getting a top 5 percent result in a half marathon
- Gaining financial freedom
- Getting to zero personal debt
- Becoming location independent
- Building a six-figure business

Over the course of ten years, Tal somehow managed to accomplish a hundred goals that usually take a lifetime to make happen. So what is it about Tal that allowed him to accomplish all of these things while most people struggle to accomplish even the smaller goals that they set for themselves? I had the opportunity to sit down with him for the podcast and so, naturally, I asked him. His response? A focus on relentless tracking of progress toward those goals.

Tal said that the number one thing someone can do

to have a better chance of accomplishing their goals is to sit down and track their progress. Why? By tracking that progress, you give yourself the opportunity to change your behavior. That's not hard, right? If you want to accomplish more, you have to take the time to make your goals measurable so that you can accurately gauge your progress and change your behavior as you go. This makes perfect sense, as tracking gives you consciousness around your performance, and that awareness is the only thing that allows you to make changes.

THE PSYCHOLOGY OF TRACKING PROGRESS

In a study authored by Benjamin Harkin, PhD, and published in the journal *Psychological Bulletin*, Harkin and his team found that regularly tracking progress toward your goal significantly increased your chances of achieving it.[1] The press release, published on the American Psychological Association website, says:

Harkin and his colleagues conducted a meta-analysis of 138 studies comprising 19,951 participants that looked at the effectiveness of an intervention or treatment designed to prompt participants to monitor their goal progress. The studies focused primarily on personal health goals such as losing weight, quitting smoking, changing diet or lowering blood pressure. They found that prompting participants to monitor their progress toward a goal increased the likelihood that the participants would achieve that goal. Furthermore, the more frequent the monitoring, the greater the chance of success.

The study also revealed that the metric you choose to track can have a significant effect on the outcome you receive. Essentially, if you choose to track your actions as they relate to your end goal, then you have a higher chance of achieving changes in your behavior itself. However, that change might not extend to the end goal that you are looking for.

If you instead choose to track progress toward your end goal rather than the individual day-to-day behavior, you might achieve your end goal without necessarily seeing many long-term changes in your behavior. What this seems to say is that being clear on the outcome you're looking for, whether that is long-term change in behavior versus the specific thing that you want to accomplish, is important when it comes to determining what metrics to pay attention to and use to track progress.

This was more or less the result that Tal found when pursuing his major goals over his ten-year window. When he tracked his goal, he saw his chances of success increase more than when he did not track them. What this meant was that tracking was a habit he had to build—success required it of him. In my conversation with Tal, I asked him about his habit of tracking, and he told me that it became a routine for him primarily while training for his full Ironman triathlon. He said that, when you want to successfully run the distance of a full Ironman triathlon, you need to be able to track every single detail of your life, such as the food you eat, the specific kinds of exercises you are doing and for how long, the amount of sleep you get each night, and everything in between. Tal believed that his ability to track his activity was one of the most important reasons he was able to achieve as many goals as he did during a short amount of time.

The good news is that this incredible power of tracking is available to all of us. We don't have to set lofty goals or pursue astonishing bucket list items, and we certainly don't have to spend the next ten years trying to complete a hundred goals. All we really need to do is keep track of our activity and progress toward the things that we want in our lives.

In Chapter Three, we talked about how to identify what it is you want for your life. The process we covered there is meant to guide you down the path of finding the changes you want to make in your life. Then in Chapter Four, we walked through how to perform a life audit to get a better understanding of your current reality and activity, and build a plan for moving forward toward the goal you identified.

Now, we'll use the power of tracking to slowly change that behavior by becoming aware of it and, as a result, start to make significant progress toward the things we actually want. This trifecta of understanding what it is we want, auditing where we currently are, and then tracking our behavior in order to change it and move us toward our goal is the secret to making big changes by taking tiny leaps each day.

HOW TO SET UP A TRACKING SYSTEM

So how do you go about actually tracking your progress toward the goals you've set and building a system that allows you to consistently move forward every day? You'll need to do a few things:

1. Define success.
2. Identify milestones.
3. Create daily routines.
4. Show up.

Define Success

Naturally, before you can determine whether or not you are making progress on your goals, you first need to know what success means. That might seem obvious, but many of us say that we want to accomplish something without fully understanding what success looks like and when we have achieved it. Thankfully, if you use the S.M.A.R.T. framework that we discussed in Chapter Two, the goal you've set should be specific enough to clearly communicate what success looks like.

For example, if I set a goal of losing ten pounds by September 27, I can very clearly understand what success for that goal looks like. If September 27 comes and I've only lost three pounds, I can be confident in saying that I failed at achieving that goal. On the other hand, if my goal was simply to "lose weight," it would leave me with more questions than answers. What kind of weight? Does losing muscle mass count? The lack of specificity in the goal would make it difficult for me to track, which would determine whether or not I was successful.

For Tal, one of his goals was to have a top 5 percent finish in a half marathon. A goal like this has a clear statement of success built into it, which allows him to effectively determine his accomplishment.

Identify Milestones

Now that you have a clear understanding of what success looks like, the next step is to break it down into a series of individual milestones that you can work toward in a measured amount of time.

Often, we don't make progress on our goals simply

because the goal itself seems challenging enough to intimidate us from taking any action. The solution to this problem is to simply break that goal into sub-goals that are more manageable. By making progress on those sub-goals, you can ensure that you are always moving forward, and eventually, the larger goal is accomplished during the process. To do this effectively, you should think of your goals as a set of accomplishments rather than one single accomplishment.

For example, if I had a goal of running a marathon next year, I might get overwhelmed at the thought of it. After all, I don't even enjoy running right now—how am I going to run for twenty-six miles? But if I took the end goal and broke it down to a series of milestones, let's say first running a 5K, then two or three 10Ks, then a few half marathons, all of a sudden I can clearly see how it might be possible for me to get to that end goal given enough time. To accomplish your goal and accurately track it, approach it with the same milestone-based philosophy.

Create Daily Routines

The next step in our process of creating an effective tracking system is to break down the milestones we've identified into the daily routines and activities that will allow us to get there. To do this, we need to look back at the concept of influence points—activities that are superior to others in terms of driving results toward our goal—that we briefly explored in the last chapter. First, you should identify which activities and habits have the largest influence on your ability to accomplish each of your milestones. Once you've figured those out, you'll then need to map them into your daily routine.

Let's look at the same goal of running a marathon. The key milestones I identify look something like this:

- Run a 5K race.
- Run two 10K races.
- Run three half marathons.
- Run a full marathon.

Then, if I identify the influence points that would allow me to best approach my training, they might be:

- Strength training
- Running
- Nutrition

After I've identified those influence points, I can then sit down and create a plan of action for each week based around those areas that I know are the most important. This might look something like:

- Lift weights 3 times per week.
- Run 5 miles each day during the week.

- Do 1 long run (10-15 miles) at least once per week.
- Eat a nutritious diet with plenty of greens and protein.

The goal with this example isn't to create an accurate training plan, it's to show that by developing a plan around consistently hitting my influence points, I've created a weekly routine that could become a habit. This routine would then dramatically increase my chances of achieving the overall goal of running a marathon.

Show Up

Once you know what success looks like, identified your milestones, and created a routine you can follow, all that's left is for you to show up every day.

It might seem too simple, but that's all that is required at this point. If you've taken the time to create clear milestones and build routines that lead to your goal, you are virtually guaranteed success so long as you keep showing up and following the plan you created.

Tiny Leap

The most important thing you can do to
accomplish your goals, no matter how crazy
they may seem, is take the time to track them

consistently and make decisions accordingly. Set up a tracking system that virtually guarantees success as long as you keep showing up.

CHALLENGE

Select one of your major goals (one of the ones that scares you a little bit!), and use the process above to break it down into milestones and build a system for consistent progress. Spend at least three days following that system as part of your routine.

PART II

WHY WE GET STUCK

CHAPTER SIX

WHY WE DON'T DO WHAT WE KNOW WE SHOULD

Where there is power, there is resistance.

—*Michel Foucault*

There is no change without movement. I and a million other "self-help" people can give you the framework to accomplish your goals. You can take all the time in the world to decide what you want and audit your reality, but without actually changing your behavior, things will stay exactly the same. You might even be worse off because you *know* why you aren't where you want to be but are still powerless to do anything about it.

Even worse, what if you do change your behavior but immediately slip back into old habits? It can seem like a painful cycle that is impossible to break. No matter what you try to do or change in your life, unless you take charge, nothing will ever happen. Instead of worrying about your potential for failure, let's try to figure out why so many of us never even bother trying.

WHY WE DON'T TAKE ACTION

Why is it that we don't do the things we know we should do? How is it that we can know exactly what to do but be unable to get ourselves to do it? These are tough questions to answer. There are many factors, but let's focus on two important ones:

- Our beliefs
- Our biases

Our Beliefs

We all carry a set of beliefs with us everywhere we go that we've adopted over years of navigating life with a unique set of experiences. Beliefs shape our views of the world, ourselves, our worth, and even what is possible. For example, if we believe we aren't worthy of change, then we will never take the kinds of actions that someone who believes the opposite might take. This isn't exactly a fair system because it means that someone who has beliefs that are suited to improving their life will automatically have a massive leg up on the person who doesn't. The good news is that it is possible to change your beliefs to better match the outcome you want to create.

But before we look into that, let's take a look at why our beliefs drive our behavior so much in the first place. Humans have survived as long as we have by fitting ourselves into groups. During our hunter-gatherer stage, we lived in groups because we knew that it would increase the likelihood of survival. As a natural side effect, we adopted beliefs about the world that prevailed within the group in the same way that our beliefs today are shaped primarily by the people we surround ourselves with. This is part of the reason that people tend to divide themselves by ethnicity naturally and why people tend to spend their time surrounded by others who are like them. By surrounding ourselves with people who have similar beliefs, we are able to quickly understand the basic tone of the group and fall into place, allowing us to define who we are and where we fit in. As a result, we act in accordance with the beliefs defined by the group and then we take actions that are consistent with those beliefs.

If we go back to our hunter-gatherer roots, it was also likely that straying from the beliefs of the group could have led to being removed, virtually guaranteeing the chance of death. This could be a reason that we tend to divide ourselves based on beliefs, because in the past, doing anything other than that could have ended your life altogether.

What we believe will drive the actions we take, which will drive what we are capable of experiencing in our lives. As such, if we aren't careful to consistently analyze and improve our beliefs about the world and our place in it, we may find ourselves sabotaging any chance of success before even having a shot at making things happen.

Our Biases

There are many different psychological biases that have a much larger effect on us than we realize. We discussed one such bias—the status quo bias—in Chapter One. It is the human tendency to hold the things and people we know in much higher regard than anything new, even if that new thing turns out to be better for us. Put simply, we like things to stay familiar, and any deviation from that status quo is perceived as a loss, even if it's positive.

This is huge if your goal is to change your life because it means that, by default, you will be wired to do nothing at all and sabotage your possibilities. It gets even more terrifying when you realize that this bias you have might actually be causing you to make poor decisions without even knowing it.

Have you ever had an opportunity to do something that could have been good for you and chose not to? Maybe in the moment you told yourself it was because you weren't qualified or were too tired, but how do you know that it wasn't just a human desire to keep your life exactly the same? This bias rears its head in decision making on both a conscious and a subconscious level. Sure, we say we want to make more money, but when it comes to taking the actions required to accomplish this, it will always feel easier and better not to do so.

What this means for our success in goal setting is that, if we can be aware of this bias, we can consciously make decisions that don't feel the most comfortable with the knowledge that our resistance is there only because of the bias. When you combine these two factors—the tendency to place ourselves into categories that determine our status quo, and the tendency to base our behaviors on how they relate to that status quo—you can get a clear picture of what makes it so difficult to change your life. So the natural question is: How can we break out of these traps and start to make progress on the things we want most?

HOW TO GET YOURSELF TO TAKE ACTION

Use Your Why

In Chapter Three, we talked about the importance of finding a strong emotional and personal why that could help you when things got difficult, allowing yourself to step outside of personal beliefs and biases and focus instead on the negative side of not accomplishing a goal. Your why, when created properly, is a powerful tool for driving yourself forward regardless of how you feel or what your fears are. It can serve as the extra bit of gas you need to propel yourself forward whenever you are stuck. Constantly remind yourself of your why.

Self-Reflection

So much of what makes us into the people we are comes from the parts of ourselves that we don't know are there. Our beliefs about the world are often hidden beneath the surface, and the biases that drive so many of our decisions may go unnoticed for much of our lives. Even though these parts of our lives may not be things we completely understand, they do still control our behaviors in significant ways. That's why it's our job to find them, understand them, and use that understanding to allow ourselves to take the actions we know we should.

The best way to do this is through self-reflection, or psychoanalysis, in the form of therapy and journaling. Psychoanalysis is the process of better understanding the subconscious beliefs we hold by bringing them to the surface. One approach to making this happen is through unfiltered sharing, which is often done through therapy. You may not intend to talk about certain things, but in an attempt to fill up an hour of silence each week, deeper meaning tends to get pulled to the surface.

Journaling works similarly because it forces you to go with the first thing that comes to mind rather than filtering until you find something you consciously approve of. Being able to better understand these subconscious beliefs and biases will allow you to create tools that can help you surpass them.

Tiny Leap

> Free writing is a great exercise for tapping into some of the subconscious thoughts we are holding on to that are driving our behavior. Try opening up a Word document or a journal, setting your timer for ten minutes, and writing everything that comes to mind no matter how ridiculous or absurd it might seem. No erasing, no stopping to think, just thoughts to page.

Just Get Started

It's always much more difficult to start something than it is to keep that thing going. This, as discussed earlier, is due to the forces of friction that are involved in the process. When you first start something, you have no real context as to how difficult it might be, how long it will take, or how much effort will be required. As a result, the uncertainty creates a resistance to starting, which can also be referred to as mental friction.

When you do eventually start and build a mental picture of what's involved in the activity, it becomes much easier to keep going because, even if it's painful, it's at least a recognized pain. Context matters, and getting started is what you need to do in order to get that context. So how do you go about just getting started? After all, if it were that easy, you wouldn't need this chapter at all.

In her book *The 5 Second Rule*,[1] Mel Robbins talks about a trick she discovered that makes it a bit easier to just get started. "The 5 Second Rule" is the idea that if you count backward from 5 and then focus on taking any physical action, it will force your brain into shifting states and make it easier for you to get started on what you need to do. Once that shift happens, you then have a small window where your focus is on the physical act of just doing something without thinking. As an example, let's say that you want to do something as simple as getting yourself to drink more water throughout the day. Maybe you struggle with it because you find it difficult to get up multiples times throughout the day and fill your glass or bottle. With the 5 Second Rule, the next time you feel that resistance, you simply close your eyes, count 5, 4, 3, 2, 1, and then immediately stand up.

Many of us experience an enormous amount of fear

and emotion when trying to convince ourselves to do something, especially something new. The 5 Second Rule has worked wonders for thousands of people around the globe, and it could work for you as well. More important than any specific tricks or strategies, you need to have a willingness to understand and confront the real reason behind your hesitation to act. Knowing the reason for your lack of action can be one of the most freeing things.

Tiny Leap

Commit to using a tool like the 5 Second Rule for one activity that you struggle with. Maybe it's getting out of bed in the morning, drinking more water, getting to the gym, or being more productive. Whatever it is, use the rule in those moments when you are resisting and see what the results are. Do this for three days to start forming a habit.

CHAPTER SEVEN

HOW TO STOP PROCRASTINATING

You may delay, but time will not, and lost time is never found again.   —*Benjamin Franklin*

Do you have a goal you've been putting off? Maybe your boss has tasked you with completing an important project? Or perhaps you need to do some major chore around the house? Whatever your goal is, if you're like most of the population, you probably haven't started yet. In fact, according to studies performed by Piers Steel, a professor of organizational behavior and human resources at the University of Calgary's Haskayne School of Business, 95 percent of the population is affected by procrastination at some point, with 20 percent of that population being marked as chronic offenders.[1] I personally fall into the latter category.

While in college, I routinely delayed my work until the very last minute. I would go to class and have a major project assigned, then I would proceed to ignore it. I'd find excuse after excuse for why it didn't need to be started just yet. Finally, the night before the project was due, I'd be forced to stay up late trying to get it done just so that I could turn it in half-baked.

Obviously, this wasn't ideal or sustainable.

The immediate gratification of not having to worry about it was nice, but the stress and anxiety felt as the deadline approached, the very real-world effects caused by turning in a subpar project, and the emotional damage done by engaging in an unhealthy habit cost far more than it was worth. I remember a time in particular when I was assigned a major project in both my drawing and my painting classes due by the end of the week. The smart approach would have been to make a plan and work on each project little by little in order to get my best work done with as little stress as possible.

Like I said, that would have been the *smart* thing to do.

On Day 1, the day I was assigned the projects, I went back to my dorm and did absolutely no work on them. Days 2 and 3 followed a similar pattern, while I worked on other—less important—tasks and completely ignored my main assignments. Finally, the night before the projects were due, I was forced to act, but by this point, the anxiety I felt was overwhelming. I knew I had to get them done, but I just couldn't conceive how this was possible. Despite the anxiety, I moved to action. Five and a half hours later, I still wasn't finished. Two more hours and finally, I had everything done. The projects weren't great, but they would do. Guess what happened next.

Because I was so tired and went to bed so late, I overslept.

I missed my first class and, as a result, had to turn in my work late. I made the second class, but the work I turned in was noticeably subpar, especially when it was hanging on a wall being critiqued along with everyone else's work. Did I get it done? Sure. But had I just worked on it a little each night, I would have given myself the chance to create something worthwhile, I wouldn't have missed my first class, and I would have felt better about myself overall instead of feeling anxious.

Given these negative experiences nearly all of us face, why do we procrastinate?

One of the most popular episodes of my podcast is based on a five-part series titled "Why Stop Procrastination?"[2] Originally authored by Celestine Chua from the website *Personal Excellence*, the series completely flipped how I viewed procrastination, and since then it has given me a basic framework for my own system. To understand it, we first have to understand *how* we procrastinate.

TWO TYPES OF PROCRASTINATION

Active Procrastination

Active procrastination is something you do when you are excited by your task at hand, but instead of channeling that excitement into a focused beam that allows you to start taking action, you find other activities that seem productive and do them instead. For example, let's say that you want to start a business, but instead of focusing on trying to land your first client, you spend time creating social media accounts or building a website. The act of creating an online platform seems like it's productive. After all, those things can often lead to clients, right? In reality, though, you know there are faster ways to get your first few clients and you are choosing to focus on other methods.

Or perhaps you want to lose a few pounds. That's a perfectly fine goal, but what if instead of cleaning up your diet, you focus all of your efforts on going to the gym? Again, the act feels productive, but it's not the most important thing you need to be doing. The danger with this kind of procrastination is that, while it can feel beneficial in the moment, it doesn't actually move you any closer to your goal.

Passive Procrastination

Passive procrastination is something you do when you aren't interested in or excited by what you are trying to accomplish. In this scenario, rather than setting aside time each day to work toward completion, you avoid all activities that are related to it. This often leads to feeling bad about yourself, which can then reinforce the cycle and cause you to procrastinate even more.

Let's say you really need to balance your budget and get a better understanding of where your money is going and when. Maybe you open the spreadsheet you'll be using but pretty soon you find yourself watching random YouTube videos. Before you know it, the time you had put aside for this important task has been eaten up and it starts to bleed into other activities. The real danger with this kind of procrastination is that, even though you aren't actively working on the task, it is still taking up mental space and pulling your attention away from the things you are working on. This kind of procrastination can also lead to increased stress and anxiety and overwhelm you as the task drains your mental resources.

WHY WE PROCRASTINATE

There are two main reasons we procrastinate: a lack of interest, and self-doubt.

Lack of Interest

Passive procrastination is most often associated with a lack of interest or passion for the task ahead: You just *don't care* all that much about what you have to do. But these things still need to get done, so how exactly can we push through when we don't have an interest in the task ahead? There are, of course, many ways to navigate this, and what works for you is going to be unique to your personality, but the underlying principle will be that you need to do one of two things: You need to find a way to either (1) generate interest and enthusiasm for the project, or (2) follow Nike's advice and just do it.

If you decide to go with the first option and try to generate some interest, you'll need to take time to reframe the activity in terms of any positive thing you can find. This could be as simple as thinking about the personal benefit of doing the task, or the fact that having a semi-mindless task allows you to take a mental break.

After our family had just moved to the United States when I was in third grade, I attended a school in Queens, New York. My teacher tested us regularly on spelling, and I always found it incredibly boring to study for. However, it still needed to be done if I wanted to get a good grade, and so I invented a game for myself to make it more interesting. To play, I crumpled a piece of paper up into a ball and threw it high into the air. Then, as the ball fell back toward me, I said the one letter of the word I was trying to spell. If I caught the ball and got the right letter, I'd throw it in the air again and say the next letter. If I missed the ball and it fell to the floor, I had to start all over again. If I misspelled a word, I had to start all over again. If I made it all the way to the end of the word, I would immediately start on the next word with the next throw.

It was a simple game that I could play anywhere, and it worked really well. Studying for my spelling tests became much more interesting, and I even used this game when practicing for the school spelling bee. I don't remember if I won, but I do know that this simple little game did wonders for me. I even adapted it for other things I needed to memorize. If you can find a way to create a simple game around your "boring" task, it can increase your level of interest.

If you decide to go the second route and push through it, you'll want to do the best you can to eliminate distractions and put yourself into a zone. One strategy I personally employ is called a pomodoro. The *pomodoro technique*[3] is a time-management method developed by Francesco Cirillo back in the 1980s. The idea is to set a timer (often in the shape of a tomato, hence the name) for twenty-five minutes. Once it's set, you should give 100 percent of your focus toward the task until the timer runs out. Once it does, you can take a five-minute break and then repeat. Combining the pomodoro with some of my favorite music has always enabled me to dial in and focus when I need it most. Whichever route you choose to take, approach it with the knowledge that it is very possible to push past a genuine lack of interest.

Self-Doubt

So you have a task. You know that you want to complete it and want it to be successful, but there is some part of you that feels like maybe you aren't qualified or shouldn't be doing it. I get it. I've been there.

But something I try to remember whenever I feel that is: Self-doubt is often caused by a lack of confidence in your ability to live up to your own or to others' expectations. When we are excited about a goal, we tend to overcomplicate things and make it bigger in our minds than it needs to be. Maybe we even start telling people what we're working on, and their expectations add additional pressure to the situation. Once this happens, we get overwhelmed, and instead of slowly taking action on our most important task, we look for adjacent activities that allow us to feel productive without addressing the fear we feel. Or worse, we collapse under the pressure of the situation and end up doing nothing at all.

There are two incredibly effective methods I've found to beat self-doubt-induced procrastination. The first is to remove the pressure off the situation entirely. Something that finally motivated me to start writing this book, despite the enormous amount of self-doubt I had, was recognizing that it didn't need to be a bestseller or win any awards. I was afraid to write it because I felt that, if I was going to do it, I'd better do it right and make it big. This, as you can probably imagine, put a ton of pressure on me and on what the book needed to be. It wasn't until I relaxed and started focusing my efforts toward getting the book to simply exist that I was able to start writing. If you can find a way to remove or reduce the pressure you feel around the things you really want to do, you'll find that self-doubt stops having the air it needs to breathe and grow.

The second method, by comparison, is counter to that idea. If for some reason you find that it's too difficult to remove the pressure, or that it doesn't help, your next option is to increase the pressure from the other direction. Remember: People will do more to avoid pain than to gain pleasure, which means that people will choose to embrace the lesser of two pains if given the choice.

An easy example of this is what happens when a deadline looms closer and closer. Many people report an increased ability to focus on the task the closer the deadline gets as the pressure increases. After all, there are consequences tied to missing the deadline that far outweigh the fear of completing the task.

Another great example is found in something my friend

Daniel did. Daniel is the founder of Gefen Media Group and he recently completed his first book called *The Self Help Addict*. I spoke with him for my podcast, and when asked how he got himself to finish the book as quickly as he did, he spoke about putting pressure on himself by telling his then nine-year-old son that the book was going to be a special gift on his tenth birthday. That's a heck of a motivator. All of a sudden, Daniel was stuck between the pressure of self-doubt and the pressure of letting his son down. Naturally, he chose the lesser of the two pains and got the book done with plenty of time to spare.

So if you find yourself struggling with self-doubt and procrastinating because of it, your answer to moving forward lies in either reducing the pressure you've placed on yourself or increasing the pressure placed on completing the task. Either will work, but until you do something to give yourself more confidence, you'll continue to find yourself struggling.

HOW TO BEAT PROCRASTINATION

A better understanding of the reasons for procrastination has given me a lot of power over my ability to get things done. After all, if you know the underlying cause of your procrastination, it becomes possible for you to create a plan of action.

Imagine if the next time you felt yourself putting something off, you could simply sit down, figure out why you were procrastinating, and make a plan for how to handle it. You would have enormous freedom to get more done in less time and actually make progress toward your goals. Identifying the reason behind your behavior and creating a plan of action are the first two of four steps to beating procrastination:

1. Identify the reason behind your procrastination.
2. Create a plan of action that takes that reason into account.
3. Measure your procrastination each week.
4. Learn how to procrastinate productively.

From here, we'll learn how to apply the rest of these steps toward creating a foolproof system for kicking procrastination in the rear.

Create a Plan

Creating an effective procrastination plan is all about considering the reason behind your procrastination and developing strategies to overcome it. For example, if I know that I dislike making sales calls, and will postpone doing it, an effective plan would suggest that I make my calls first thing in the morning when my willpower is at its highest. A different plan might recognize the potential for error even with said willpower, and may bypass calls altogether in exchange for e-mails. A third plan might state that neither of these options will work based on my tendency to procrastinate, and incorporate outsourcing the work so someone else can do it.

On the other hand, if you're procrastinating on something you truly want to do like training for a 10K race, you need to find ways to eliminate the self-doubt involved with that process. Maybe your plan will have to include first training for a 5K in order to prove that you can compete. Or perhaps it will involve running the distance first to prove that you can do it. Or maybe the plan simply needs to focus on the mental side of things and will involve consistent reminders that you are good enough to do it. The point is that when you are trying to create a plan for beating procrastination, you need to clearly understand what your reason for procrastinating is and use it as the basis for tackling the issue. Your plan is less about overcoming and more about understanding the hidden factors so you can get things done.

Once you've created a plan for yourself, it's important to stick with it. After all, what is the point of a plan that doesn't get executed? As we discussed in Chapter Six, the only way change happens is if you actually do the work. Thankfully, this is where a system, a set of processes that allow you to think ahead of time so you can focus on following through, can come in handy. The benefit to following a system is you eliminate the need for will-power, decisions, and virtually all things that might get in the way of execution. You simply sit down and follow the plan.

For example, if the plan I created required me to make all my sales calls when I have the most willpower, then I would focus my efforts on quickly executing my first few tasks in the morning. A simple system for making this happen would be creating a morning to-do list: Check my in-box and answer any urgent e-mails, look at my calendar to be aware of upcoming meetings for the day, and make at least five sales calls. By making it clear what needs to happen each morning and adding sales calls to that list, I create a system that will help me execute my plan. Figure out what tasks need to be done every time, what order to do them in, and how they fit into your life.

Measure

What you measure grows. This is primarily because by measuring your results in an area, you are forcing yourself to pay attention to it, causing you to take different actions, which then improves your results. If you want to beat your procrastination, then you need to create a plan and plot it out into a system, as we've just discussed. Once you've done that, you need to execute the system consistently. Then, you need to learn how to measure your procrastination levels in order to consciously reduce and improve over time.

The best way to measure your procrastination is to keep track of how much time a task takes you and compare it to how long it *should* take you. This is something I do regularly. When I sit down to create my to-do list for the day, I'll also add rough estimations of how long the task should take me. Don't worry about this measurement being perfect—the more you do it, the better you will get at guessing. Once you've added the estimated time, you can sit down, put on a timer, and begin. Then record the amount of time it actually took you.

The difference between the two times can, of course, be caused by a number of factors, but it should at least give you a better idea of how much time was wasted. Be sure to record that number, so that you have something to measure against next time. By completing an exercise like this, you will naturally improve your performance while becoming more conscious of your actions.

Productive Procrastination

The final step to tackling procrastination is to recognize that procrastination doesn't necessarily need to be a bad thing. Often, when we procrastinate, it's simply because our bodies and minds need to step back and take a quick break. That could last a few minutes or a few hours, but as long as you are able to get back to the task eventually and get it done, it shouldn't be viewed as a problem.

In addition to this, we often put off working on things because we need a bit of time to fully process what is required for the task. Putting it off doesn't mean that we're never going to do it, but it does allow us to come to the task with a much clearer understanding of what needs to be done rather than jumping right in. I call this process *productive procrastination*, and it's important that you learn to recognize and separate it from what we've just discussed.

Unlike regular procrastination, which comes from a desire to avoid the task, productive procrastination comes from a desire to put yourself into the best position to make it happen.

Productive procrastination, while it may feel the same in the beginning, can be one of the best things we do to complete a task with the best results. But if we treat it the same way we do regular procrastination, it can trigger a cycle of self-doubt and frustration that actually turns into real procrastination. Give yourself the room to procrastinate sometimes and try to understand why you are pushing the work off—doing so will enable you to put a system in place or take advantage of the positive effects without fear.

Tiny Leap

Procrastination is one of the biggest productivity killers out there, and it often stems from a lack of interest or crippling self-doubt. If you can identify the reason for your procrastination and build a system around it, you can get yourself to take action even when you don't want to. Additionally, if you learn to identify productive procrastination and separate it from the rest, you can use it to your benefit.

CHALLENGE

What was the last thing you procrastinated on that led to negative consequences? Take this time to figure out what your reason for procrastinating was and think about what you could have done differently. Next time you have a task to complete, use the four-step process to avoid procrastinating.

CHAPTER EIGHT

THE FOUR SINS OF PERSONAL DEVELOPMENT

Only a fool learns from his own mistakes. The wise
man learns from the mistakes of others.

—*Otto von Bismarck*

As we navigate life and start to take charge of the things
we want, we are going to be faced with quite a few hurdles.
In this chapter, we'll explore some common obstacles, or
as I refer to them, the four sins of personal development,
and how they can be avoided or overcome to ensure you're
changing your life in the most efficient manner possible.
The four sins are:

1. Comparing ourselves to others
2. Lying to ourselves

3. Focusing too much on the end goal
4. Losing track of the end goal

Comparing Ourselves to Others

Growing up, I constantly gauged my own success on how it compared to those around me. When I ran track in high school, I would base my performance in a meet on whether or not I got first or second. First? Great, I did well. Second? I screwed up. Less than second? Well, you'd find me upset in a corner somewhere. When I took a test, it was all about what the other students got. When I worked on a project at my job, I regularly paid attention to how hard I was working compared to my coworkers. There was never a moment in which I measured my success or failure compared to my previous performances. In fact, I could always outperform my previous personal bests, and still be upset if I didn't come in first or at least perform well in comparison to everyone else.

While this kind of competitiveness is sometimes okay—and often promoted to kids—it causes some serious issues in adulthood. Imagine, for example, how psychologically and emotionally damaging it would be if we based the success of our weight loss goals on whether or not we lost more than some other person. That would be absolutely absurd. Or what if we determined the value of our lives compared to the people we see on platforms such as

Instagram? Both of these scenarios are a recipe for disaster, but unfortunately that's exactly what many of us do. We identify what we want, audit our lives, start making progress, and then compare that progress to our friends or our support group or random people we see online, leading to discouragement, depression, and a cycle of guilt that causes us to slide back into old behaviors before ever having a chance to create real change.

So why do we do this? Recent studies on the behavior of small groups of people working together in both collaborative and competitive environments have shown that we humans do, in fact, have a predisposition to consistently compare our own performance with that of those around us. One study authored by Marco K. Whittmann and his team and published in the research journal *Neuron* found results that suggested that this need to compare ourselves to others potentially dates back to our need to fit into a group.

If we think back to our hunter-gatherer nature, it's clear that humans are remarkably social beings. Sure, some of us may be introverted and others might be extroverted, but in order to ensure our survival, humans have developed the ability to form close bonds with those around us. In fact, those close bonds are often the number one reason that we've been able to survive. One theory derived from these findings is that our desire to compare ourselves to the people around us is a necessary trait for becoming part of a community. If that's true, then it makes perfect sense that we compare ourselves to each other. After all, if a simple comparison between my performance and yours is all that it takes to determine social hierarchy, then naturally, it would happen constantly.

So how do you overcome something you're hardwired to do? The key seems to be in first understanding where that desire comes from, and then simply making a conscious decision to stop yourself when it happens. Comparing ourselves to those around us, and more important, comparing our successes and failures to those of others around us, is a *habit* just like every other habit.

And just like every other habit, that means it can be reprogrammed. We can, through taking tiny leaps each day, create a new habit that allows us to compare our successes and failures to ourselves, rather than to those around us. Doing this will allow us to pursue the goals that we have created without the fear of underperforming as compared to our peers. We will also avoid the incredible disappointment and depression that can come with the constant comparison of our lives to those of people we know only in passing.

Lying to Ourselves

Because we humans can view things only from our personal perspectives, we have a warped view of the world around us and our place in it. Unfortunately, we are limited to having just five senses—sight, hearing, touch, taste, and smell—that act as our means of experiencing and interacting, so every single piece of data that makes it to our brain is being filtered. This creates a natural bias that we each carry around with us and live by. While not necessarily a bad thing, it does mean that our personal experiences are not 100 percent accurate.

The biases we carry around with us are intended to guide us through life and protect us from harm. We instinctively categorize things as good or bad, thanks to our hunter-gatherer roots. We default to routines and habits as a way to reduce the cognitive strain that would be required otherwise. We take our experiences and build principles or routines around them in order to create the same results or avoid negative consequences. But that also means that we aren't always making the absolute best decisions available to us. This is why ideas generated by a group of people are often better than ideas generated by one person. The additional filters and biases get brought into the equation to create a larger, and more accurate, picture of reality. Our perceptions are sometimes flawed, which creates an ability to lie to ourselves, and it's why having outside accountability, whether through a partner or through tracking, is a *major* factor in creating change.

We want to believe the best version of ourselves that we can. In fact, we need to believe the best version, and as a result, we tend to exaggerate or misrepresent ourselves when tracking progress toward our goals. Lying to ourselves is one of the biggest mistakes we engage in to hold ourselves back. It might seem like a simple thing, but without a precise view of our activity, we make poor decisions based on biased information.

For example, if you want a piece of chocolate cake, or if you want to buy something new, you might think back on your behavior and come to the conclusion that it should be okay because you've been eating well and going to the gym or you have been budgeting properly. But do you know the exact number of calories you consumed? Do you know exactly how much will be burned at the gym that night? Do you really know how much came out of your bank account this week? Are you adding in the $25 you spent on random purchases? The goal is not to obsess over details, but to understand that when you are making a decision based on the bias you have of your own behavior, you aren't thinking clearly. Things may work out fine, but a lack of clarity can lead to making decisions that set you back dramatically.

Focusing Too Much on the End Goal

Another mistake that people make is focusing too intensely on the end goal. When we do this, we create two big negatives:

First, we judge successes and failures based on how close we are to achievement. This may not always be a problem, but it can cause a lot of discouragement and in some cases procrastination or a lack of action altogether, especially if you set large goals.

Second, every day that you have not achieved your goal becomes a failure.

Over and over again, we set very large goals for ourselves. Things like wanting to become a millionaire, wanting to own a private jet, and other very large and audacious (usually financially motivated) goals. Now, the fact that we set very large goals is a good thing. But it becomes a problem when we wake up each day and gauge our progress toward those large goals. Because often, the goals that we're setting for ourselves are things that cannot be accomplished in the next ten to fifteen years. When you are setting goals at that level, it does you no good to check your progress toward them each day. Doing so will only lead to frustration, anxiety, and depression.

Additionally, judging success based on proximity to the goal causes us to think short-term instead of long-term. We end up trying to score a win so that we can feel better about ourselves, and by doing so, we make snap decisions, moving us farther away from the goal, and farther away from developing key habits to get us there. This is especially a problem because achieving a large goal is all about thinking and acting with the long term in mind.

Here's a perfect example: Let's say that you want to drop a few pounds. If you're thinking short-term, you might decide to cut back on your calories and eat just enough to get by each day. You might then add in extreme workouts that are difficult to do but create results. These actions will result in you dropping a few pounds and, *voilà*, your goal is accomplished. However, the actions are not sustainable. When people lose weight this way, they often end up gaining it back as soon as they stop doing the routine. Just look at the results of the TV show *The Biggest Loser*. The whole point of the show is to push people to their extremes in order to create extreme weight loss. This makes for excellent TV, but often after a contestant has successfully completed the show, they end up putting back on the pounds once they go back to the real world. Instead, if you go about it with a long-term view, you recognize that the secret is to create a routine and strategy that you can live with for the rest of your life.

Lifestyle changes create long-term benefits, so while they're not as sexy, they do get you the results you're looking for and they allow you to maintain those results. Approach a goal with a long-term vision and focus your efforts on the day-to-day process that will eventually lead to achievement.

Losing Track of the End Goal

On the other hand, the final obstacle that keeps us from achieving what we want is completely losing track of the goal. This happens every year with New Year's resolutions—we sit down and set goals for ourselves, things we *really* want to accomplish, then forget what we were working toward a few months later. As we learned back in Part One, if we don't know where we are trying to go, we will never be able to take the actions required to get there.

One of the most common lessons that life coaches and personal development experts teach is that we should write down our goals and put them in front of us so we're constantly reminded of what we are trying to do. Imagine if you were trying to drive across the country to a town you've never been before. What's the first thing you would need in order to get there? Likely, you would need a car, maybe some clothes, some food and supplies, and of course, you would need a map or GPS of some kind. After all, if you're trying to go to a specific place, you can't just drive in any direction and hope you end up there. But if on that drive across the country, that town disappeared off the map, maybe because of some kind of extraterrestrial invasion, your GPS would stop working and you'd have a much harder time getting there.

When it comes to personal development and change, your goal can be thought of as the town you are trying to reach and the actions you take each day are your GPS, your directions, your map. In the same way that if the town were to randomly disappear off the map you would have a harder time getting there, if you were to forget what your main goal is, you might still accomplish it by stumbling around in the dark, but it would be much more difficult than it needed to be.

By placing your goal somewhere that you're sure to see it every day, like on a Post-it Note around your home, you automatically increase the amount of time spent thinking about it, causing you to naturally look for opportunities that can move you toward measured progress.

These four sins—comparing yourself to others, lying to yourself, focusing too much on the end goal, and losing track of the end goal—are the most common reasons you might get derailed from achieving what you want. Learning to avoid these obstacles can move you forward consistently while experiencing fewer setbacks along the way.

Tiny Leap

Changing your life can be difficult and has plenty of challenges attached to it. Instead of adding to those challenges, try to avoid common pitfalls by learning what they are and being aware of how they could affect you.

CHAPTER NINE

ON THE NEED FOR MOTIVATION

People often say that motivation doesn't last. Well, neither does bathing—that's why we recommend it daily.

—Zig Ziglar

One of the main reasons that social media has caught on in today's world is because it allows us to consistently experience a life we aspire to have. When we look at a travel blog and read about all the exotic locations the blogger visits, we live vicariously through them while at the same time feeling motivated to pursue more of that in our own lives. Unfortunately, that spark wears off pretty quickly and often doesn't lead to any real action, and so we end up back on the platform looking for another glimpse.

When talking about personal development and changing your life, the topic of being motivated enough to take action is often discussed. Usually it's because someone doesn't have enough of it, and if they could just be a little more motivated, they'd *definitely* accomplish all the things they say they want.

"I do want to get out of debt—I just need a little bit of motivation." I would argue that this isn't actually the case. Sure, it might seem like motivation is what you need to get off your butt and do the things you know you need to do, but if we look closer, it's likely that there is a bit more to it than just that.

One major issue with relying on motivation in order to move your goals forward is that it's often short-lived. Take a photo of a beautiful beach that you find on Instagram, for example. First, you consume it, experience a spike in your motivation levels, and maybe even start to take some initial action toward the goal of traveling more. A few minutes later, things start to level back out. Maybe, while you were on that high, you looked for plane tickets to plan a trip, but the minute the motivation wore off, you quickly came crashing back to reality and never followed through. This isn't always the case—there are some periods in which the motivation lasts a bit longer and you start taking serious action, like the random moments of inspiration found in the Six Stages of Personal Change. But do you really want to base your ability or inability to change your life completely on something as fickle as motivation, which may or may not show up?

A second issue with motivation is that, often, it's not the core of the problem. In an article titled "Your Problem Isn't Motivation"[1] published in the *Harvard Business Review*, Peter Bregman makes the argument that, while motivation may seem like the big issue, more often the problem is a lack of follow-through. He says that, as long as we care about something, we are, in fact, motivated to do it. So as long as we care about something, trying to solve the problem of not "being motivated" will only cause more frustration, procrastination, and decrease our likelihood of acting. Peter's argument is that instead of looking for motivation, we should solve our lack of follow-through. So how exactly do you do that? Let's take a look at a quote from Peter's article:

Motivation is in the mind; follow-through is in the practice. Motivation is conceptual; follow-through is practical. In fact, the solution to a motivation problem is the exact opposite of the solution to a follow-through problem. The mind is essential to motivation. But with follow-through, it's the mind that gets in the way.

That last line is hugely important for our purposes. Motivation happens internally, but follow-through requires physical action. Often, being too internal, or relying too much on motivation, is the thing that gets in the way of our ability to take action.

I think back to my conversation with two-time X Games gold medalist and half-pipe world champion Jen Hudak when she said, "If I didn't turn my mind off right before a run, I wouldn't be able to perform my best." Her words hold the secret to getting out of the motivation trap and creating follow-through. The solution is to shut down your thoughts and allow yourself to take unfiltered action.

USING INCENTIVES TO IMPROVE FOLLOW-THROUGH

Dan Pink, author of the bestselling books *Drive* and *To Sell Is Human*, gave a TED talk[2] on the role that incentives play in helping us solve problems. In it, he brings up a psychological study known as "The Candle Problem."[3] Created by Karl Duncker at some point in the middle of the twentieth century, the study sought to discover the role "functional fixedness" plays when trying to solve problems. Participants were given a candle, a matchbook, and a box of thumbtacks. Their task was to find a way to light the candle and attach it to the wall without letting any of the candle wax hit a table that sat below. The correct solution is to empty the box of thumbtacks, use the tacks to pin the box to the wall, and then place the candle inside and light it. Simple, right? It seems like it should be obvious, but most participants struggled with the task, using the match to melt the side of the candle to stick it against the wall, or trying to tack the candle itself to the wall.

The interesting part of the study is that Duncker and his team found that when people were given the same items but the thumbtacks were presented separately from their box, the problem became easy to solve. The reason this happened is because of functional fixedness. This cognitive bias causes people to view objects primarily in the way they were intended to be used, without considering other options. In other words, when we are presented with an object that has a clear function, we tend to categorize it as such in our minds, making it more difficult for us to view the object in any other capacity.

When participants received the box with tacks in it, it was categorized as a vessel for the tacks. When they received the box alone, it became an additional tool they could use. This kind of fixed thinking happens quite a bit in our regular lives as well—in fact, it's the entire reason that life hacks and DIY repurposing furniture have gained popularity. The idea of taking something that was meant for one thing and repurposing it for another is inherently interesting because it opposes the functional fixedness we all experience daily, creating the "Wow, I've never thought of that!" response.

So what does functional fixedness have to do with

motivation and incentives? This is where it gets interesting. Incentives tend to cause a similar effect on our view of options as functional fixedness did in these participants.[4] When we incentivize ourselves, or others, to accomplish a specific goal or perform a task, it can narrow our focus to the end point. This phenomenon can be used to our advantage if we are struggling with procrastination and just need to get a task done. By clearly defining the actions required and then incentivizing the execution of those actions, we can narrow our focus and reduce the friction required to accomplish the task. The drawback is that by narrowing our focus, we sacrifice creativity and the ability to react flexibly if something goes wrong.

This is why incentives tend to work best when tackling very particular things that have a specific solution attached to them such as flossing, putting together reports at work, or getting out to the gym. Tasks like these are purely execution focused with no "on your feet" thinking to throw you off. Unfortunately, when it comes to changing our lives or accomplishing major goals, there often is not a specific path or solution involved, and instead requires an open mind and a unique approach that might be stifled in an incentivized environment.

If this is the case, the best solution is to create a follow-through system that will make it easier for you to take action while having the space to change your strategy when necessary.

THE POWER OF A FOLLOW-THROUGH SYSTEM

When Gary Vaynerchuk, the founder of VaynerMedia and VaynerX, decided that he was going to get his physical health under control, he didn't sit on Instagram and watch videos of athletes or read inspirational quotes. He was already plenty motivated. Instead, he looked at his issues around follow-through and designed a system that would solve those problems and allow him to succeed. He identified what he wanted, audited his reality, and then created a plan to change it. Sound familiar?

His solution? To hire a fitness and nutrition coach that would travel around the world with him and force him to fix his poor habits. After taking the time to audit himself and better understand the reason behind his poor follow-through, he realized that, in every area of his life where he was motivated and effectively following through, he was always accountable to another person. Knowing that about himself made it simple to decide to put someone in charge of his health so he was accountable to someone else and, as a result, start following through. Don't worry—your system doesn't need to be as insane, or expensive, but you should learn from Gary. You will absolutely need a system if you want to start taking more action on the things you are motivated to do.

The Queen Bee/Worker Bee System

Chase Reeves, one of the founders of a business education platform called Fizzle, once explained the concept of the Worker Bee and the Queen Bee as it relates to freelancers and anyone trying to build a business by themselves. Here's how it breaks down: A freelancer needs to do a million and one things in order to service clients and continue growing at the same time. It's a challenging balance to find, but the Queen Bee/Worker Bee framework can help us understand how to get it done.

The idea is to separate your time into periods of wearing different hats. For example, when you are wearing the Queen Bee hat, you are completely focused on strategy-based tasks, growth activities, selling new clients, and anything that will keep your business growing. Then, when you put on the Worker Bee hat, you become focused exclusively on executing that strategy and servicing your existing clients. It seems a little silly on the surface, but by creating this clear separation between the two roles, you are allowing yourself to focus on a task at hand without the distraction of the other things that need to get done.

This is a follow-through system that allows you to remain productive as a solo producer, and the simplicity of it means that it can be adapted to become your follow-through system for anything you are struggling with. If you want to pay off your student loans, put on your Queen Bee hat and create a strategy that works for your lifestyle needs. Then switch roles, put on the Worker Bee hat, and do nothing but execute. Follow the system— that's all you need to do.

But this system isn't completely foolproof. After all, one of the main things stopping you from executing might be that you have too many ideas. That's certainly a good issue to have but can lead to indecision and increased anxiety about how to prioritize. My solution here has been to develop the habit of writing everything down. Whenever new ideas come to mind, I jot them down as soon as I can in order to get them out of my head and move forward, without fear of forgetting or losing the idea. If I haven't created a strategy for anything yet, then having a list will allow me to directly compare ideas and decide which is the best to pursue based on what is most important to me in that moment.

By taking the time to create a system for your follow-through rather than hoping for motivation to show up or adding incentives that do more damage than good, you guarantee that you'll always be able to take action regardless of your mood or what position you are in.

Tiny Leap

Motivation, while it often seems like the solution to our problems, is relied on too much when it comes to getting ourselves to do the work. Additionally, this desire is usually misplaced. Motivation, in the way we think about it, is very likely not the core issue to begin with, and incentives, while effective, aren't applicable to all scenarios. Focus instead on a follow-through system for your goals so you take more action regardless of whether or not you are particularly motivated that day.

CHALLENGE

Select one of your goals and apply the Queen Bee/ Worker Bee follow-through system to it. Create the strategy ahead of time and then focus exclusively on execution.

CHAPTER TEN

THE PASSION PIT

Patience and time do more than strength or passion.
—*Jean de la Fontaine*

Growing up, I wasted a lot of time trying to find my passion. If I could just find that thing I was most passionate about, everything else would fall into place. Does this sound familiar?

Over the last few years, the self-help industry has gotten very good at doing two things: convincing people that they need to follow their passions in order to be happy, and selling all kinds of products to help people figure out what those passions are. Like many who actively consume self-help content and experiment with all the different ways people tell us we can live a happier, more fulfilled life, I bought it—hook, line, and sinker. I felt that if I could just find that one thing I was meant to do, that thing I loved most, everything else would fall into place. Not only that, I also knew in my heart of hearts that once I did find this thing, it would always be exciting to work on it. There would be no frustration, no lack of motivation. I would simply enter this zone of complete flow anytime I sat down to work. The problem with this, as you probably know, is that passion has virtually nothing to do with the level of happiness and fulfillment we have in our lives.

Cal Newport, author of the bestselling books *So Good They Can't Ignore You*[1] and *Deep Work*, spent years looking at the correlations between passion and job satisfaction. What he found is that there are four key characteristics shared across all the people who are truly fulfilled by their work. These four characteristics are a sense of autonomy, a sense of mastery, a sense of connection, and a sense of impact.

The first three of those characteristics match up quite nicely with something called the self-determination theory.[2] Originally developed by psychologists Edward L. Deci and Richard M. Ryan, this theory of motivation is concerned with supporting our natural or intrinsic tendencies to behave in effective and healthy ways. It states that there are three basic psychological needs that must be met to support well-being and mental health.

Competence

The first is competence, or what Newport calls a sense of mastery. When we are highly skilled at something, we tend to enjoy doing that thing more, because of the sense of control and accomplishment it provides us. Think about the last time you did something that felt effortless. Perhaps it was a particularly good workout at the gym, a successfully completed task at work, or a meal you cooked without a recipe. Whatever it was, it probably felt really good while doing it because things happened seamlessly. That's what competence or mastery in a skill feels like—an unfiltered ability to execute a complex task with no additional effort required. The sense of control we feel also expands our options with the task and our ability to think creatively, which has been proven to increase our overall happiness levels.

Relatedness

The second psychological need is relatedness, which is what Newport calls a sense of connectedness. Humans are naturally social creatures who want to operate in a flock or small tribe. Introverted or not, we all crave connection to other humans and our group, a need that is rooted in our early hunter-gatherer days.

As a result, we tend to feel a greater sense of connectedness to the work we do or the things we do in our personal lives if we can find a group for it. For example, if you feel close to your coworkers and are able to connect with them around the shared experience, you are more likely to feel a sense of satisfaction toward your job even when things get frustrating. The need for relatedness or a sense of connectedness, when met, tends to improve the bond we have to our work overall and decreases the desire to walk away.

Autonomy

The third need is autonomy, which is exactly what Newport calls it. Autonomy or freedom is dramatically important when looking at how "happy" you feel in your workplace. This is because autonomy gives you ownership, and ownership gets you invested in the outcome. The need for autonomy is one reason why remote-work opportunities or unlimited vacation policies are so popular at companies. By increasing your sense of control over how you spend your time or how you tackle your projects, these opportunities allow you to feel more connected to your job, which can have positive effects on your satisfaction.

These three needs, as outlined by the self-determination theory, when integrated into your life or your career, create the foundation for maximum growth, fulfillment, and happiness.

Impact

Cal's fourth requirement, a sense of impact, while not represented within Deci and Ryan's model, is no less important for creating a connection with your work or goals. We've always wanted our work to have meaning. Whether that work is going out to find food for survival as our ancestors did or redesigning the user interface for a piece of software that people use every day, we want our work to matter. The more we can create that meaning, the more connected we will feel to the work we have to do.

Note that none of these requirements include the word "passion." So why is the quest for passion often presented as a requirement for happiness and fulfillment? I recently looked at Google Trends data for the keywords "follow your dreams" and "follow your passion." Since the data dates back to 2004, I saw that the interest for both keywords was quite low at that time. However, if you look at the trend data for today, there is a clear rise in interest over the years. What this implies is that prior to the self-help and career industries starting to use these terms as end goals, people cared less about finding their passions and more about working hard at the opportunities in front of them.

At the beginning of this chapter, I mentioned that, growing up, I spent a lot of time looking for my passion. I thought, if I found it, I could dedicate all my time to it, become extremely skilled, and create a life that I was excited to wake up for every day. As a result, I experimented with as many things as I could, thinking that I'd eventually stumble upon my passion. I would recommend that you spend as much time experimenting and trying new things as you possibly can. This experimentation will lead to finding something that you enjoy. But on the negative side of constant experimentation, you never spend enough time on one thing to develop any level of mastery, one of the psychological principles of true fulfillment, which leads to a lack of autonomy and connection to others.

So using Newport's characteristics and the self-determination theory as a framework, the answer seems to be *don't search for your passion*. In fact, you can't search for your passion. Even if there were something you were passionate about today, that position would change over time as your interests changed. Instead, look for the opportunities that are right in front of you and then make tiny leaps each day to meet the four requirements above.

THINK LIKE AN IMMIGRANT

When my dad moved to the United States, his first job was picking apples in an orchard during the fall season. As you can imagine, this was not the most glamorous or stable position. Outside of the prime picking season, most workers were laid off because they were no longer needed. My dad wasn't passionate about picking apples and he certainly wasn't passionate about a job that could let him go at any moment, but it was an opportunity to establish a foothold in the United States, make connections, and pave the way for his family to move here with him. So regardless of his passion, he took the opportunity. That decision paid off tremendously.

A few months into his time there, he made the right connections, which led him to a full-time position as a line worker at a local juice bottling plant. Again, this was not the most glamorous position, or what he was passionate about, but it was an opportunity that gave him enough stability to move my mom, my sister, and me from Jamaica to live with him again. While at the plant, he put in the time and developed his skills. He learned the ins and outs of the machines, and often sacrificed time with his family to make himself more valuable, which eventually led to his being promoted multiple times and establishing a deeper relationship with his boss.

Fast-forward a few years: His boss left the plant for a better position at a different company, and he arranged for my father to be offered a better position as well. At the time of my father's death, he was a quality control manager in charge of his own team, in a role that paid him more than the average American salary, and doing work that he felt passionate about. My father did not pursue or chase his passions. Instead, he looked at the opportunities in front of him, developed his skills, attained a degree of mastery in his role, and built relationships with the people around him.

These choices allowed him to build the life he wanted, earn the kind of money he wanted, and gain passion for his work while simultaneously providing for his family in a way that many other fathers are not able to. The life I live today is a direct result of the choices that he made in those early days. That is the power of chasing opportunity, rather than passion.

What opportunities are in front of you right now? What chances do you have that you may not be paying attention to? For my father, being an immigrant to the United States and starting over with nothing meant that he needed to take the opportunities that were directly in front of him and use them to create the things he actually wanted. You don't need to be an immigrant to have the same results. All you need to do is stop putting so much focus on finding your passion and start focusing on creating opportunities for yourself. Build skills, become valuable to the marketplace, and you'll start to find that your work and your life become much more interesting regardless of what you do.

Tiny Leap

"Follow your passion" is a common message that creates a lot of frustration and uncertainty among people who embrace it. The truth is that the enjoyment you feel for your career has very little to do with passion. Instead, chase your opportunities and focus on developing mastery over a skill and increasing your value to the marketplace.

CHALLENGE

Identify and list one to three moments in your life when you weren't necessarily passionate about what you were doing, but they led to enormous benefit later on. Then, list one to three opportunities that are in front of you right now. Are any of these worth pursuing in order to create the life you want to live?

PART III

HOW TO KEEP MOVING FORWARD

CHAPTER ELEVEN

CHOOSE YOUR STANDARDS

Acceptance of prevailing standards often means we have no standards of our own.

—*Jean Toomer*

Tony Robbins has made a name for himself by breaking down the keys to improvement into their fundamental parts. One of the main keys? Higher standards. In an article titled "How to Raise Your Standards,"[1] Tony says:

What happens when you decide something is an absolute "must?" What happens when you cut off any other possibility than you succeeding—when you decide that you are either going to find a way to make something happen or you'll create the way yourself? When you raise your standards and turn "should" into "must," you are making an inner shift to take control over the quality of your life.

Most of us live our lives with a long list of "shoulds" that we want and "shoulds" that we feel pressured to want. The "shoulds" that we want are our goals for ourselves that embody the type of life we want: We should lose weight, we should be present in our relationship, we should make more money.

The second kind of "shoulds" are ones that society puts on us but are nothing more than other people's expectations: We should become a lawyer, we should get a stable job, we should get married. These two types of shoulds are a part of everyday life, but until they become "musts," they will likely never happen. When we take the shoulds and turn them into musts, they start to take shape and become a part of our lives.

Turning any should into a must, though, requires something special—a kind of alchemy that allows you to add form to your ideas and transmute them into gold. And rest assured, if you want to accomplish any of the goals you have set, you'll need to learn how to perform that alchemy and transform your should-haves into must-haves that drive you forward. So what's the secret ingredient?

To turn a should-have into a must-have, you need to raise your standards for yourself, your life, and the world around you. So what, then, you might ask, is a standard? The standard you have is the base scenario that you are willing to accept for yourself. It's the cost of entry before anything else can be considered. Everyone has a standard. It may not be something we are conscious of, but we do have it. For example, let's say you show up to work every day, put in the time, and then go home. That's a standard that you hold yourself to subconsciously. Every day that you are expected to, at the bare minimum, you will show up to work and put in the time.

Your standard may not even be one that you are choosing to hold yourself to—always showing up to work may have been placed on you by external forces. After all, if you don't show up for work, you may lose your job. Since you don't want to lose your job, you adhere to that standard. Here's another example: What time do you wake up in the morning on workdays? If you are like many Americans, you wake up with enough time to get ready and head out to work. This is an external standard that has been applied to your life for you. The time you wake up is dictated by when you need to be at work.

The more conscious you can be with the activities you engage in, the better off you'll find yourself when it comes to making good choices for yourself. This concept holds true in relation to our standards as well, so the first thing you can do to become aware of the standards you hold yourself to is to choose them yourself, instead of letting external forces determine them. Doing this doesn't need to be difficult; it can be as simple as choosing to wake up an hour earlier than usual, which will allow you more time in the mornings to do what you want rather than just waking up for work. It's a choice that creates a standard for yourself based on what you want rather than what your job demands.

This plays out across all areas of our life. Most of the way we live our lives is based on reacting to the standards others have set for us, rather than proactively creating standards by which we want to be held. Learning to consciously choose these standards is an easy way to feel more in control of your life and have ownership over the decisions you make.

Tiny Leap

The quality of life you live is often based on the level of standards you allow yourself. These standards can be placed there by others or they can be consciously chosen. Only once you decide to raise your standards and then create a strategy to hit those standards will you be able to create change.

CHALLENGE

If you currently set your alarm to wake up just in time for work, try setting it one hour earlier and doing something to work toward a personal goal with that extra time.

CREATE YOUR STRATEGY

On the surface, Erin Newby lives a life many would envy. She has a dream job as a product designer—a role that just a few years ago she didn't know existed—at one of the largest and most influential companies in the world in New York City, a city she grew up dreaming of. She makes great money and is on her way to being debt-free. And she is slowly but surely building a career as a conference speaker. Not bad for a young black woman who grew up in less than ideal circumstances.

Given the trajectory of her life, it would be easy to think that she should be content with her position. But when I asked her what her plans were for the future, she said, "I'm not sure, but definitely something even bigger." Erin grew up with the kinds of hardships that result in only one of two outcomes: a crushing defeat, or an unsatisfiable drive. She learned that the difference between the two often comes down to the strategy you employ and how you employ it, as discussed in one of the most impactful books she has read thus far titled *Good Strategy, Bad Strategy*, by Richard P. Rumelt.

"It made me realize how little I tend to think about my strategy in life," she said. She explained that immediately after beginning the book, she looked back on her life and understood that she was where she was because she unknowingly had a good strategy. As Steve Jobs once said, you can only connect the dots when you look backward. Just like Erin, most of us don't spend a lot of time thinking about our strategy. Sure, we want to make more money, maybe we even set a S.M.A.R.T. goal and change our day-to-day behavior, but what is our overall strategy for accomplishing the goal? Many never stop to answer this question, and some never even consider this question at all.

In Part One, a very basic process is outlined for you to change virtually anything in your life and move in the direction you want to go. It's designed to be easy to jump into with very little holding you back, but if you want to create lasting change, and if you want to do it in less time, at some point you are going to need a real strategy. Here's how the complete process works:

1. Decide what you want.
2. Audit yourself.

3. Create a strategy.
4. Change your daily behavior.

So what exactly is a strategy? And how exactly do you come up with one? Your strategy is the overarching approach you will take to accomplish the things you want. Unlike tactics, which can also be thought of as day-to-day behavior changes, strategies encompass everything that you do. For example, let's say that your goal is to make more money. For Step 1, you simply need to decide what it is that you want. You'll also need to choose your standards, and decide what your "must-have" is. For Step 2, you'll need to audit yourself. For the above goal, we might look at our salary and any other random pieces of income we have, add them all together, and come up with what our annual total income is every single year. This audit gives us a better understanding of where we are.

Step 3 is the new piece of the puzzle and requires us to create a strategy. By taking what we've determined is our goal, refining it to be more specific and follow the S.M.A.R.T. format, and then getting a better understanding of where we are in relation to that goal, we give ourselves all the tools we need to create a strategy. If we want to make more money, our strategy might be to try and get a raise at the end of the year. This would help us understand that our approach to making more money is to get a raise. Of course, we will have to understand what exactly is required to get that raise—maybe our boss just wants us to do a little bit more work; if that's the case, we know that if we put in enough overtime, we should get a raise at the end of the year.

Or maybe what our boss actually cares about is some kind of financial result for the company, so if we can find a way to increase the company's revenue or save money, we'll be more likely to get the raise. The key here is to identify what the approach should be in order to create the outcome that will accomplish our bigger goal.

Moving forward, let's pretend that our boss *is* looking for some kind of financial result from us. Now, we can write out all the things we could do to increase the company's revenue or save the company some money. This is our list of tactics, which detail the strategy. It's made up of the specific things we can do and work toward in order to create the desired result, and they're contained within our overall strategy of increasing the company's revenue or saving money. Then, we can use the tactics to determine our day-to-day tasks.

If we know that helping the sales team increase their revenue by providing marketable information to them is one way we can help, then our daily activity should be to keep better track of the information we send to salespeople, and spend time researching what could lead to purchases, and package it in the most effective way possible. What you end up with is this funnel that allows you to align your ultimate goals with the strategies that could get you there with the tactics required to achieve those strategies with the day-to-day activities you need to take in order to achieve those tactics. This strategy is then directly connected back to our ultimate goal of making more money by getting a raise.

HOW TO CREATE A WINNING STRATEGY

Now that you know how this all fits together, how exactly can you create your own strategy and start moving forward? It's a very simple process. The first step is to understand what it is that you want, and the second is to get a better understanding of where you are. Once you have these two pieces of the puzzle, you simply need to sit down with a piece of paper or your tablet and list all the possible approaches that could lead you to your goal. You could write "Point A" (your starting point) at the top of the page and "Point B" (the goal) at the bottom of the page. In between those points, list potential approaches to create a map. From there, your job is to pick the approach that seems the likeliest based on your current situation and the goal that you have and, of course, take the time to test it.

Tiny Leap

When trying to change your life, one of the best things you can do for yourself is take the time to create a better strategy. You'll automatically be ahead of the game.

CHALLENGE

Look at the goals you've set for yourself and use the Point A to Point B approach outlined in this chapter to create a step-by-step strategy for hitting that goal.

CHAPTER TWELVE

FAIL YOUR WAY FORWARD

Success is not final, failure is not fatal, it is the courage to continue that counts.

—*Winston Churchill*

When I first got into podcasting, I launched a show called *Time to Launch*. The goal was to help people who wanted to create something interesting without quitting their full-time jobs. On the show, I interviewed some incredibly interesting entrepreneurs and nine-to-fivers about what they did to manage their time and still get their projects done. But after about two months of doing the show, I decided to end it because a few things had become really clear for me.

First, I realized that the show I had created was not one that I was interested in continuing. Sure, it could possibly be helpful for other people but it just wasn't very enjoyable to create. Second, the show wasn't catching on in the way that I wanted it to. I had a few listeners here and there, but no single episode ever broke over fifty or so downloads. Now, I know that download numbers aren't the only metric that matters, but at the time I was heavily focused on trying to reach as many people as I could.

My first show could be considered a failure by many. It never gained any traction, and it was a show that I didn't enjoy creating. But that failure is what eventually led me to launch *Tiny Leaps, Big Changes*. From Day 1, the show proved itself to be a winner. Originally I intended to hit 10,000 downloads by the end of the first month—an absolute stretch of a goal considering my second podcast, *Casual Conversations with Awesome People*, ran for about three months and generated a total of 12,000 downloads.

My next stretch goal for *Tiny Leaps* was to hit 30,000 downloads by the end of the second month. Finally, I wanted to hit 100,000 downloads by the end of the third month. I remember chatting with my friend Mark Moriarty, the founder of Awesound, the podcast-hosting platform I used at the time, and telling him that there was no way that I could possibly hit those numbers. But then something incredible happened.

Ten days into the show launching, I hit my first 1,000 downloads. Not bad, but at that pace I was only going to hit about 3,000 downloads by the end of the first month.

Then, the very next day, I hit another 1,000, and the day after that I hit my third 1,000—3,000 overall downloads in just the first twelve days. On Day 15, I'd hit my 10,000 download stretch goal in half the time. I knew that I had landed on something that was resonating, but I still didn't fully understand how well it would be received. Six weeks after I launched my podcast on January 1, 2016, it crossed the 100,000 download mark. This was astonishing. I had set a stretch goal for myself of hitting 100,000 by the end of my third month fully intending not to be able to hit that goal. In just six weeks the show had crushed that number with no signs of slowing down.

I'm telling you this because my first podcast didn't do well. I didn't enjoy creating it, no one listened, and I shut it down after just two months. To me, it was a failure. My second podcast did slightly better, but it still wasn't that fun to create. Then finally, after learning how things worked, and how to create a good show, I launched something that resonated in a big way. I often hear that the number one thing that holds people back is a fear of failure, and while I understand the reason for this fear, I also wish that it was possible to reach through this book and remove that fear from you completely.

Because the truth is: Failure isn't a bad thing.

In fact, failure is an absolute requirement for any level of success that you might aspire to. If you want to lose weight, you're going to fail at staying consistent until you finally get it right. If you want to make more money, you're going to have to embrace the possibility of being broke and in debt. You'll need to struggle until you finally get it right and learn how to do it. If you want to have a better relationship, you're going to have to go through breakups and fights, and argue until you get it right.

Life is not easy, and nothing is handed to us on a silver platter. But there's one sure-fire thing you can do to guarantee that you always get more of what you want: Simply embrace the fact that failure will forever be a part of your life. Whether you choose to be ambitious or not, you will still fail. The difference is in what that failure leads to.

At the Maharishi University of Management Class of 2014 commencement, Jim Carrey told the story of his father, whom Jim described as someone who could have made it in comedy and accomplished his goals. But rather than go for that dream, his father chose to go the safe route. Fast-forward a few years and the company that he dedicated his life to decided to simply let him go. Jim shares this story through pained words, but at the end he leaves us all with a message that is worth repeating. He says, "My father taught me a great many things, but most of all he taught me that you can fail at what you don't want, so you might as well go for what you do want."[1]

He's absolutely correct. One way or another, you are going to fail, whether you go after the things you want or just go through life day by day. So why not let your failure push you to the next step rather than leave you hurting with no direction? How do you fail your way forward?

HOW TO FAIL FORWARD

Failing forward is more of a mind-set than a specific strategy, but that doesn't mean that there aren't clear steps to get it done. If you've made it this far, these steps are not going to be surprising:

1. Take action.
2. Review your results.
3. Create a plan.
4. Repeat.

Take Action

Failing forward requires that you fail purposefully. This means choosing to take actions that could end in failure rather than just letting it find you. At this point, we've covered everything from how to identify what you want to how you can track results and make changes accordingly. Naturally, these same processes apply here.

Use the simple process we discussed in Part One to identify what it is you want to do. After that, use the techniques we explored in Part Two to push past obstacles such as procrastination to actually take action. The only difference here is that when you fail, you'll know that it was an expected outcome rather than something that snuck up on you. This shift in mind-set makes a massive difference when it comes to ensuring that your failure doesn't crush you.

Review Your Results

Once you've taken action and, naturally, failed at what you were trying to do, the next step is to sit down and review your results. The concepts of tracking, auditing, and reviewing are incredibly important because, as you know, without taking the time to look at your results with an open, honest eye, you'll never see what areas there are to be improved. With every failure comes a series of lessons that, if utilized, can help you avoid the same pitfalls again and again.

To perform a review of your results, simply sit down with a piece of paper or your computer and try to list ten things you could have possibly done to avoid the failure. It's not important that you accurately guess what caused the failure. By listing a minimum of ten items, you will force yourself to think deeply about what could have been done differently. After the first three to five items, it will get harder and harder to come up with more, so embrace this struggle as it's where some of the best lessons can be found.

Create a Plan

This is the key piece of the puzzle when trying to fail your way forward. Failure, and even lessons learned, don't do anything for you if you aren't willing to get back on the horse and try again. By creating a plan of action for how you will move forward, you are pre-committing to giving it another shot, which will help you recognize that the failure itself wasn't as bad as it seemed. When creating this plan, be sure to include any lessons learned or patterns recognized from your review period.

Repeat

Failure doesn't have to mean stopping. It always frustrates me when I'm listening to a podcast and I hear the interviewer ask his guest whether or not they had ever considered quitting when things got tough. It makes no sense to me. What does that even mean?

Imagine if you were unemployed and trying to land a job. You've submitted fifty résumés, gone to five interviews, and there's one position that you think you have a good shot at landing. After your interview, you send a thank-you note to the interviewer and spend the next few days eagerly awaiting their response. About a week later, you get an e-mail back saying that, although they liked you, they decided to go in a different direction. Frustrating, right?

Now imagine I asked you, "So do you think you're going to quit?" My guess is that you'd look at me with extreme confusion. Quit? That's not even an option. After all, if you don't get a job, you won't be able to eat or feed your kids. That's what I want you to recognize. The same thing is true for virtually anything in your life at which you might fail. If you set a goal to run a half marathon and aren't able to complete the race, are you going to walk away and never run again? Of course not! If you set a goal to make more money, you start a business, and a potential client tells you they aren't interested, are you just going to shut down and accept the amount of money you currently make? No!

My point is that, as long as you still want the thing you are working toward, there is no such thing as failure. Because the only way to fail is to stop trying, and unless you are going to take a single failure and completely alter your day-to-day life because of it, you are never going to stop trying.

So learn your lessons, make a plan, and get back on the horse.

Tiny Leap

Failure is a necessary part of the formula when trying to change your life. It will happen. Accept that. Take the time to learn from your failures and then use that experience to get back on the horse for another try.

CHALLENGE

The best way to get over the fear of failure is to realize that it isn't a big deal. Go out and do something you know for a fact will lead to failure, like asking the cashier at a store for a 10 percent discount regardless of whether or not they are offering them. They will likely say no, but do it anyway and embrace the failure.

HOPE

We must accept finite disappointment, but never lose infinite hope.

—*Martin Luther King Jr.*

Ever since I was thirteen and first discovered the world of personal development through a Tony Robbins book called *Awaken the Giant Within*,[1] I knew that one day I wanted to write a book of my own. I wanted to inspire others to change their life in the way that Tony had inspired me. It's been a dream of mine ever since and I knew that one day it was going to happen, so much so that I spent a lot of time in my teens picturing the moment when that book was released to the world. I had this weird little fantasy about packing my family up into a car on the day the book was released, driving them to the closest bookstore, and pointing out mine on the shelves. I've always envisioned hearing my sister lovingly make fun of me, my mom saying "Good job," and my dad asking me to explain why the book wasn't in the front of the store, his face beaming with pride.

Unfortunately, that dream will never come true. At least, not in the way I'd always imagined it. Just three months into the writing process for this book, my father passed away suddenly. But I don't want to talk about his death. Instead, I want to talk about the last five months of his life.

In June 2017, Hopeton Lloyd Clunis Sr. was diagnosed with Stage 2 lung cancer. He had been a smoker for nearly fifty years but had suffered absolutely no health issues as a result, so the news came as quite a shock. The doctors told him that, because of his impeccable health outside of the cancer, he had a good chance of beating it and prolonging his life. He was a proud man. He worked hard, never asked for help, and stuck to his ways. But after hearing these words and realizing there was hope, my father made radical changes in his life almost overnight. Within a month he quit smoking—a part of his life for fifty years—completely. He had tried quitting multiple times unsuccessfully but yet he was able to do it immediately in this situation. It didn't stop there.

He spent more time with his family. He started eating healthier and cut out foods he had spent his entire life loving. For the first time, he took off from work to gather the strength required to deal with treatment. About two months after the day he was diagnosed, a man who was so stubborn that he wouldn't even try "new" foods changed everything about his life.

That kind of change doesn't happen easily and most of us will never experience it, or if we do, it might come in the form of a desperate attempt to reconnect with our younger selves during a midlife crisis. It's the kind of rapid change that causes you to question your identity or, at the very least, happens *because* you are questioning your identity. So if most people never undergo extreme changes in the way he did, it leaves me asking the question: How was he able to do it? Which driving force was behind his ability not only to figure out what he needed to do, but to execute it quickly and make those changes stick?

The immediate answer that comes to mind is fear. After all, he had just received a diagnosis for a disease that is usually fatal. A disease that, even if he had managed to survive, would forever change his quality of life and his ability to provide for himself or his family. Surely he made all these changes because he was afraid of that reality, right? Because he was naturally trying to move away from that pain by accepting the lesser of two pains.

Fear probably did play a role, but I have a hard time believing it was the only driver behind those changes. After all, if it was only fear, wouldn't he have made these changes sooner? If fear is the belief that something is dangerous, he was well aware of the dangers of smoking. So why didn't that fear drive him to make changes before it was too late? I don't think it was fear alone. I think it was hope.

As with most cancer diagnoses, there was a lot of confusion around what stage he was in. After a few weeks of tests and back-and-forth, the doctors finally told us that it was considered to be Stage 2. Not a great result, but certainly not the worst it could be. Of course, the doctors never told him that he was guaranteed any result, but they presented the options to him, and in those, he saw a chance that he could make it through. He found hope.

That hope allowed him to make dramatic changes to his life virtually overnight and make them last. It allowed him to endure two massive, and life-threatening, surgeries. It allowed him to deal with a burned-up esophagus as a result of radiation treatment. It allowed him to deal with a level of poisoning from chemo that, alone, often causes patients to wish they were dead. It allowed him to be okay with getting a feeding tube installed because his esophagus was too burned to eat solid foods.

The hope of survival accompanied him to the brink of death and kept him precariously balanced right at the edge, and then, when it seemed like he might be on the rise, hope left and he fell.

This kind of story happens all the time. Often when

someone is faced with a diagnosis that could end their life, they are willing and able to make changes dramatically. In these extreme moments, the power of hope is activated and change is possible. But what about the rest of us? Each and every one of us should be swelling with hope at all times. We have the power to change our lives, to change the very world around us. It's possible, no matter how far down we fall, for us to climb out of our holes and create the life we want.

So why don't we? Why are people who find themselves in situations like my father did able to use the power of hope as a powerful steroid for creating change, while the rest of us never move forward? The answer, I believe, lies in our perception of stakes. The concept of stakes in gambling is an interesting one that I think applies perfectly to regular life.

Let's say you've got some experience playing poker with your buddies. Nothing serious, $20 here and there, a few beers, maybe some wings. It's a fun night, and you're really good at it. Then all of a sudden you win some money and decide that you want to test out your skills in the big leagues. You fly out to Vegas, get some chips, and sit down at a table. How do you think you'll play?

In a situation like this, we often think that our skills will transfer directly to the new table. After all, it's the same game, right? If you're good at a table with your buddies, you should be fine. At the very least, you shouldn't be awful. But then you start losing money game after game. You might think that you just weren't good enough to play at this big table. Maybe the other people there were just way better than you. That assumption might be true, but it's not the only thing going on, which brings us back to loss aversion.

As we discussed earlier, loss aversion is the tendency to hold on to what we have rather than risk it for something better. In other words, we would rather protect than gain. The cool thing about cognitive biases and human tendencies is that they aren't hard-and-fast rules. For example, there is nothing stopping us from consciously choosing to risk everything in order to gain something new. We can absolutely do that, but once logic goes out the window, these biases and tendencies describe how we are likely to act. The more stressful or emotional a situation we find ourselves in, the more likely we are to fall back on one of these tendencies.

So let's get back to the table. We were great at a table with our friends, so why did we screw up so badly at this new one? Part of the answer is that the stakes were increased. All of a sudden, instead of $100 pots, we were dealing with $1,000 pots. Since you are used to pots that have much less risk involved, your stress levels are going to be higher when playing in this new environment. You are then more likely to lean on your biases and, as a result, play with the intention of not losing rather than winning.

This small shift makes a huge difference in the outcome of the game. Even if you were good enough to play at that table, the increase in stakes makes it less likely for you to win. Every individual loss will naturally feel more important than it actually is because your focus is on *not* losing. When you were playing at the small table, the stakes were small and you could take risk easily without much fear. That willingness to risk allowed you to create wins consistently and get better at the game. But owing to the size of the stakes, a win at that table didn't mean all that much. Low stakes, low reward.

Once you stepped into a higher-stakes game, it became harder to take those risks because your stress increased. Those risks, more than your skill, were what allowed you to win in the first place and so you found it harder and harder to win. Those losses then made it even more difficult to take risks, and a cycle was created that you couldn't escape from.

So what does this have to do with my dad's cancer diagnosis? When someone is facing a life-or-death situation, the world instantly becomes a high-stakes poker game. For that person and their family, the danger is all too real and losing means death. Loss aversion will kick in, but playing it safe isn't an option. In my dad's case, if nothing was done, death was certain. His only shot, the only hope there was, lay in making massive changes and taking huge risks.

Imagine you are stuck in a building during a fire. You are in a room with the door closed, the alarms are going off, and there is no exit. If you try to go through the door, the room will be engulfed by smoke and flame. Chances of survival are slim. Behind you, there is a lone window. There's no fire escape, but you can clearly see the ground five stories below. What do you do? As we've seen in many such catastrophes, often the choice people make is to go through the window. Sure, the fall could kill you, but a 1 percent chance of survival by going through the window is still better than a 100 percent chance of dying if you do nothing. My dad knew that his only shot was to make incredible changes, and fast. For the high-stakes poker player, they know that their only chance of winning is to ignore loss aversion and choose the risky path that makes winning possible.

We spend the majority of our time worrying about our day-to-day lives. We stress over conversations we've had, who likes us and who doesn't, what we'll have for dinner, and a whole slew of other things that matter only in a low-stakes environment. We do this because we believe we have time. Because we take tomorrow for granted. Sure, we know that we are going to die one day. We are consciously aware of this fact. But somehow, death always seems unrelated. We hear about tragic accidents, violent attacks, and unfortunate illnesses that claim millions of lives every single year. But we relegate these events to the "somebody elses" of the world.

In our minds, life is not urgent. It's something we have always had and we can't imagine a moment in which we don't have it any longer. But life is, in fact, urgent. At my father's funeral, when given the chance to share his parting words, one of my uncles said something that has stuck with me: "We are born to die." This is a truth that I believe we all know, but fail to realize. From the moment we are born, a countdown clock that represents the total amount of time we'll be given in this life starts. We live our lives, learn to love, age, and eventually die at a predetermined time, in a predetermined place, that we have absolutely no control or knowledge over. Death is a certainty—the only one that comes with life. But for those of us who aren't confronted by a major diagnosis such as cancer, the amount of time we have left is never made clear, and therefore, urgency is never created.

Life never becomes a high-stakes game in our minds. But what if it was? How would we live our lives if we constantly heard the tick of our own personal countdowns? Would we not live with more urgency? Wouldn't the high stakes of our lives become clearer? Wouldn't we also make massive changes the way my father did? Couldn't we also embrace risk? Wouldn't we also choose the 1 percent chance of living, over the 100 percent chance of death?

I believe we would. I hope this book has shown you that change is possible and that, by taking small actions each and every day, you can create the change you so deeply desire for your life. But now I'd like to remind you of something incredibly important.

This life we lead feels as though it will last forever. It feels like we'll always have more time to do the things we want, to create the change we are looking for. But your time is counting down, and it's closer to zero now than it has ever been before. Your only hope, your only shot at living the life you want, is to take action *now*.

Embrace risk, embrace change, and play the game with the intention of winning.

Change your life in the same way that my father did. Embrace your own mortality, recognize that you are running out of time, and use that truth to play the high-stakes poker game that your life really is. If you can do that, you can change your life in ways you couldn't even imagine.

NOTES

Chapter 1: What Is Change?

1. Kübler-Ross, Elisabeth, and David Kessler. "The Five Stages of Grief." Grief.com, 2017. https://grief.com/the-five-stages-of-grief/.

2. "Fading Affect Bias." https://en.wikipedia.org/wiki/Fading_affect_bias.

3. "Sensory Gating." https://en.wikipedia.org/wiki/Sensory_gating.

4. Nguyen, Vi-an. "Only 38 Percent of Americans Feel Fulfilled by Their Work: More Survey Results." Parade.com. https://parade.com/227302/viannguyen/only-38-percent-of-americans-feel-fulfilled-by-their-work-more-survey-results/.

5. Ferriss, Tim. *The 4-Hour Workweek*. Harmony, 2009.

6. Henderson, Rob. "How Powerful Is Status Quo Bias?" Psychologytoday.com, 2016. https://www.psychologytoday.com/us/blog/after-service/201609/how-powerful-is-status-quo-bias.

7. Potts, Richard. "Variability Selection in Hominid Evolution." February 8, 1999. https://onlinelibrary.wiley.com/doi/abs/10.1002/%28SICI%291520-6505%281998%297%3A3%3C81%3A%3AAID-EVAN3%3E3.0.CO%3B2-A.

Chapter 2: What Do You Want?

1. Doran, George T. "There's a S.M.A.R.T. Way to Write Management's Goals and Objectives." November 1981. https://community.mis.temple.edu/mis0855002fall2015/files/2015/10/S.M.A.R.T-Way-Management-Review.pdf.

2. Kahneman, Daniel, Jack L. Knetsch, and Richard H. Thaler. "Anomalies: The Endowment Effect, Loss Aversion, and Status Quo Bias." 1991. https://www.jstor.org/stable/1942711.

Chapter 3: The Importance of Why

1. Sinek, Simon. "How Great Leaders Inspire Action." TED talk, 2009.
2. "The Ovsiankina Effect." https://en.wikipedia.org/wiki/Ovsian kina_effect.
3. "The Pleasure Principle." https://en.wikipedia.org/wiki/Pleasure _principle_(psychology).
4. Hadziselimovic, Nils, et al. "Forgetting Is Regulated via Musashi-Mediated Translational Control of the Arp2/3 Complex." March 13, 2014. http://www.cell.com/cell/fulltext/S0092-8674(14)00148-2.

Chapter 4: Audit Your Reality

1. McLeod, Saul. "Cognitive Dissonance." https://www.simplypsycho logy.org/cognitive-dissonance.html.
2. Heshmat, Shahram. "What Is Confirmation Bias?" https://www .psychologytoday.com/blog/science-choice/201504/what-is -confirmation-bias.

Chapter 5: Change Your Behavior

1. Harkin, Benjamin, Thomas L. Webb, and Betty P. I. Chang. "Does Monitoring Goal Progress Promote Goal Attainment? A Meta-Analysis of the Experimental Evidence." American Psychological Association. https://www.apa.org/pubs/journals/releases /bul-bul0000025.pdf.

Chapter 6: Why We Don't Do What We Know We Should

1. Robbins, Mel. *The 5 Second Rule.* Savio Republic, 2017.

Chapter 7: How to Stop Procrastinating

1. Steel, Piers. "The Nature of Procrastination: A Meta-Analytic and Theoretical Review of Quintessential Self-Regulatory Failure." American Psychological Association. 2007. http://studiemetro

.auinstallation29.cs.au.dk/fileadmin/www.studiemetro.au.dk/Procrastination_2.pdf.
2. Chua, Celestine. "Why Stop Procrastination?" https://personalexcellence.co/blog/procrastination/.
3. "Pomodoro Technique." https://en.wikipedia.org/wiki/Pomodoro_Technique.

Chapter 9: On the Need for Motivation

1. Bregman, Peter. "Your Problem Isn't Motivation." *Harvard Business Review.* https://hbr.org/2012/01/your-problem-isnt-motivation.
2. Pink, Dan. "The Puzzle of Motivation." TED talk, 2009.
3. "The Candle Problem." https://en.wikipedia.org/wiki/Candle_problem.
4. Kounios, John, and Mark Beeman. *How Incentives Hinder Innovation.* http://thepsychreport.com/books/how-incentives-hinder-innovation-creativity/.

Chapter 10: The Passion Pit

1. Newport, Cal. *So Good They Can't Ignore You.* Grand Central Publishing, 2012.
2. Deci, Edward L., and Richard M. Ryan. http://selfdeterminationtheory.org/.

Chapter 11: Choose Your Standards

1. Robbins, Tony. "How to Raise Your Standards." https://www.tonyrobbins.com/mind-meaning/how-to-raise-your-standards/.

Chapter 12: Fail Your Way Forward

1. Carrey, Jim. Jim Carrey Commencement Speech. Maharishi University of Management, May 24, 2014. https://www.mum.edu/whats-happening/graduation-2014/full-jim-carrey-address-video-and-transcript/.

Conclusion: Hope

1. Robbins, Tony. *Awaken the Giant Within.* Free Press, 1992.

ACKNOWLEDGMENTS

As I said in the conclusion, writing and publishing a book has always been a dream of mine. With that said, I couldn't have imagined just how challenging it would be to accomplish, and I want to say thank you to everyone who has been with me on this journey.

First of all, I want to say thank you to my father. I can't fully express the gratitude I have for everything you did. Since you passed away, I have spent a lot of time looking at the person I am, and it's become obvious just how much of that is because of you. Thank you for the long conversations we used to have about the world and for always allowing me to explore my curiosities without judgment. Every viewpoint or life philosophy I have can be traced back to something you taught me, and so I want to say thank you for being a role model and someone I can be proud to have learned from.

To my mother, you have always pushed me to work hard and have always allowed me to dream big. More important, you have always been there for me when I've failed. You are an inspiration and someone I know I can always turn to.

To my family, Sherri-Ann, Jhnell, Keniesha, Garen, Kevin, Dane, Junior, my in-laws, my aunts and uncles, my cousins, my nieces and nephews, it's hard to explain just how much you've supported me throughout my life. Each and every one of you embodies the philosophies found in this book, and you have played a large role in helping me to understand just what is possible when we take action.

Rachel, you've been a source of love and support from the moment we met, and neither the podcast nor this book could have happened without your willingness to listen to and encourage my crazy ideas.

To my friends, both life-long and new, thank you for your endless positivity and for lending an ear when I needed it most.

To my brilliant editor, Hannah, and the rest of the team at Center Street, thank you for making this dream a reality. Your trust, support, and guidance have been more than I could ever ask for, and it's because of you that I've been able to create something I can be proud of.

To every single person who allowed me to use their story within this book, I say thank you from the bottom of my heart. Not just for your permission, but for making the choices you've made in your lives and for always playing to win. You are my friends and mentors, the people I look up to, and the people I want to emulate.

Finally, to all of you who are willing to share your time with me. To the people who found my podcast on Day 1 and were willing to give me a shot. To the people who have shared their stories with me, left harsh reviews, or just listened silently. I want you to know that you are my muse. When I first launched the podcast, I kicked it off with the statement that I would continue showing up if you would do the same. Not only have you shown up, but you've shared it with friends, family, loved ones, and strangers. You've taken action on my advice and allowed me to bare my soul. You are a major part of making this happen, and I cannot express my gratitude enough.

ABOUT THE AUTHOR

Gregg Clunis is a content creator and entrepreneur. He is the founder of Tiny Ventures, LLC, where he is focused on creating the education, tools, and resources to help everyday people improve their lives. He's the host of *Tiny Leaps, Big Changes*, a top-ranked self-help podcast that makes personal development simple. Gregg is passionate about understanding why people do the things they do, utilizing design thinking to solve complex problems, and sharing his personal experiences with others in the hopes of having a positive influence.